CW00969602

FRANK LLOYD WRIGHT'S

TALIESIN AND TALIESIN WEST

To Jim

*this is a small token to say a
big thank - you*

Sandra X

FRANK LLOYD WRIGHT'S

TALIESIN AND TALIESIN WEST

KATHRYN SMITH

WITH PHOTOGRAPHS BY JUDITH BROMLEY

HARRY N. ABRAMS, INC., PUBLISHERS

Again, Taliesin! When I am away from it,

like some rubber band stretched out but ready to snap back

immediately the pull is relaxed or released,

I get back to it happy to be there again.

Frank Lloyd Wright, *An Autobiography* (1943)

CONTENTS

L I F E

It is impossible to separate Taliesin and Taliesin West from the life of their creator, Frank Lloyd

Wright, America's best known and most highly esteemed architect. With the exception of his

early childhood, a twenty-four-year span as an adult between 1887 and 1911 when he was living

in either Chicago or Oak Park, Illinois, and trips in pursuit of his work, Wright could be found

in either a verdant valley in southern Wisconsin or on a mesa below the McDowell Mountains, in

Paradise Valley, Arizona.

The son of Anna Lloyd-Jones and William Carey Wright, he was born on June 8, 1867,

in Richland Center, Wisconsin, only twenty-two miles from where Taliesin is located. His mother's

parents and their sons and daughters, immigrants from Wales, homesteaded near Spring Green,

just south of the banks of the Wisconsin River. Although he had an itinerant childhood as his

father moved from town to town seeking employment as a minister, eventually the family returned

to Wisconsin and settled in Madison. This move began one of the most important chapters in

Wright's life — when he was taken from home by his mother's brother, James, to spend his summers

on the family land. The energetic imagination of the boy was exposed to the fertility of the farm,

the underlying order of nature, and the strong will and determination of the Lloyd-Jones family.

This experience would have a lasting impact with consequences that would unfold throughout the

remainder of Wright's life.

The center of life at Taliesin and Taliesin West revolves around work in the drafting room — producing drawings, now aided by computer, fabricating models, composing specifications, and meeting with clients, engineers, and consultants. In this view, Wright, accompanied by Kenn Lockhart, puts the finishing touches on the model for Monona Terrace, a civic center planned for Madison, Wisconsin.

By contrast, his life as an adult was formed in the urban setting of Chicago, where he ventured at the age of twenty to seek employment as an architect. Within two years, he would be married and living in a house of his own design in the suburb of Oak Park, bordering tranquil countryside near the Des Plaines River. While his independent practice, established in 1893, grew and prospered, he took advantage of the cultural life of the city. He could be found in concert halls, at the theater, in the art galleries, and in the bookshops; his love of classical music, drama, Asian art, literature, and fine printing were developed and refined at this critical juncture.

The Oak Park period, which produced six children in rapid succession and a revolutionary approach to domestic and commercial building that influenced modern architecture for the remainder of the century, ended abruptly in 1911, when Wright returned to southern Wisconsin. The ostensible reason was the unfavorable publicity that surrounded his affair with a former client, Mamah Borthwick Cheney, and his wife's refusal to grant him a divorce. But with the construction of Taliesin in the valley his grandparents had originally settled, Wright produced a building that would signal a distinct shift in his sensibility and justify the break with his suburban practice.

It is clear that Wright needed the close contact with nature that an agrarian existence offered; and within this setting, he established his architectural workshop. For the next twenty-six years until the construction of Taliesin West – with the exception of travel associated with his practice and a period of forced exile – Taliesin was the center of Wright's idyllic world. Within the studio, new buildings came forth in drawings and models; on the farm, the crops were tended and harvested; in the house and gardens, he was surrounded by his art collection, his books, and music.

This life was augmented and expanded with the founding of the Taliesin Fellowship in 1932. Giving formal structure to circumstances that had been in place for many years, the Fellowship was an apprenticeship program where young men and women could work with Wright – side by side – in the drafting room, on construction sites, and in the fields. By this time, he had gained a sympathetic new partner in his wife, Olgivanna, and a second family with the birth of their daughter, Iovanna, in 1925, and the adoption of Svetlana, Olgivanna's daughter by her first marriage.

In 1937, Wright began to build a new Taliesin on the outskirts of Phoenix, thus establishing a migratory pattern between Wisconsin and Arizona. While both contained a house for Wright's family, a studio, living quarters for the apprentices, and communal rooms for dining, music, and the projection of films, they were a study in contrasts in every other way. Taliesin was sited overlooking lush, contoured farmland, whereas Taliesin West was butted up against the sharp features of the arid desert; Taliesin evoked protection with deep, hovering roofs, while Taliesin West seemed ephemeral with only translucent canvas overhead. The stimulation of these contrasts sustained and nourished him until his death on April 9, 1959.

Until her death in 1985, Olgivanna Lloyd Wright presided over the school and architectural practice that Wright left behind. In 1940, Wright had established the Frank Lloyd Wright Foundation; it is now the parent organization over the Taliesin Fellowship, which includes today the Frank Lloyd Wright School of Architecture and Taliesin Architects.

After spending part of the day in his study with his correspondence or polishing the manuscript of a book, Wright would go into the drafting room to approve or revise drawings. Often an audience would gather around him when he sat down at a drafting table to sketch out an idea.

The life of the farm was essential to the rhythm established in Wisconsin. Wright's formative experiences on the Lloyd-Jones farm were relived as he worked the land for a third generation. At the height of his financial prosperity, in the 1950s, Wright owned a majority of the land that had previously been under cultivation by his uncles and grandparents.

Work in the studio or in the gardens was regularly interrupted by a break for refreshments. "The tea circle is symbolically placed in the general plan of Taliesin," an apprentice explained in 1936. "It is just halfway between everywhere, even meals. Blocks of stone, set in concrete, form the seat which encircles a large oak tree making [a] stone terrace garden, with a small pool of water at the center."[1] In this view, Ludwig Mies van der Rohe is seen in 1937 with, left to right, Wright, Olgivanna, Maginel Wright Barney (Wright's sister), Hulda Drake, and John Lautner, standing next to the tree.

From the earliest years of the Fellowship, the review of apprentice work has been known as the Box. "Twice a year the apprentices were required to produce designs of their own for the Christmas and Birthday Boxes," Herbert Fritz explained. "One apprentice designed and built the box that held the drawings – always beautifully crafted with a unique hinge or opening and closing device. On the occasion of reviewing the drawings all apprentices grouped around Mr. Wright to hear his comments."[2]

Celebrations at Taliesin and Taliesin West involve all members of the community, and none is more exhausting nor more satisfying than the annual Easter breakfast, which takes almost a week of preparation. The focus of activity at Taliesin West is the cooking of an Easter bread called baba and the assembly of pascha cheese, both traditional Russian confections Olgivanna Lloyd Wright knew from her childhood. The week begins with the delivery of one thousand eggs — most to dye and place on the tables or to hide for the egg hunt, some for the baba, and the remainder for the pascha cheese. The centerpiece of the table is the baba, which requires among its ingredients thirty pounds of flour, three hundred egg yolks, and eight pounds of butter. Two days of cooking commence with the separation of the three hundred eggs on Friday morning.

Activity mounts during the day until the bread comes out of the oven late in the afternoon. The tall cylindrical loaves, their paper forms removed, are gently lifted onto pillows and slowly rocked from side to side until cooled.

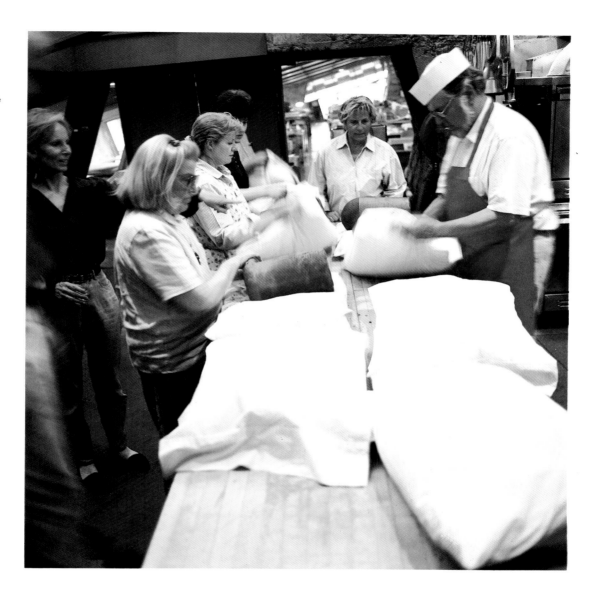

Members of the Fellowship and guests dye six hundred hard-boiled eggs and shine them with vegetable oil in readiness for decorating the tables. Neighbors, friends, family, and other guests come from nearby Phoenix as well as from all across the United States.

With the baba as the centerpiece, the tables are set for Easter Sunday breakfast in the Apprentice Court.

Wright had a vivid memory of the bounty of Lloyd-Jones picnics in the valley, occasions usually initiated by his uncle Thomas. He carried on this custom, both in Wisconsin and Arizona, with the Taliesin Fellowship.

Former apprentice Edgar Tafel remembered, "On Sunday morning when there was no chapel – in spring, summer, and early fall – by about 11:00 or 11:30, we'd assemble in the tea garden for a picnic trek. The cooks had already prepared everything – their homemade cakes were especially good – and we had salads and cans of milk, homemade ice cream, our own butter and buttermilk."[3]

During the summer in Wisconsin, the Fellowship often gives an elaborate outdoor party to entertain friends and neighbors. The pond, fields, and pastures are transformed for one magical evening. One of the most memorable of these occasions took place in August 1955, when, after weeks of preparation, a party was presented on the theme of Marco Polo's return from Asia. After the guests were seated, a boat sailed across the pond and up to the dock, and Fellowship members dressed in appropriate costumes disembarked.

As Marco Polo approached, he was followed by attendants carrying party favors such as silk scarves. In this view, Frank Lloyd Wright is seated at the right with his wife, Olgivanna, while their daughter, Iovanna, passes among the guests with gifts.

On another occasion, in September 1951, the party had an Arabian theme. Here Frank and Olgivanna Lloyd Wright are escorted on a ride by the pond in a feathered coach.

Between 1950 and 1970, the Fellowship presented performances of music and dance under the direction of Iovanna Lloyd Wright, accompanied by music composed by her mother, Olgivanna. Beginning in 1957, these performances were staged in the Pavilion at Taliesin West and were known as the Festival of Music and Dance. Eventually musical plays were given with costumes and lighting and stage design created by members of the Fellowship. This scene is from the dance drama *Time Upon Time,* which was held in 1969 and 1970.

These costumes were also designed and made by the Taliesin Fellowship.

Come forth into the light of things — let nature be your teacher.

Motto of the Hillside Home School

ORIGINS

The Lloyd-Jones family, Frank Lloyd Wright's maternal ancestors, made an indelible mark on the physical site and intellectual character of Taliesin. Wright spent every summer of his youth on the family farms, and his childhood memories rooted him for a lifetime to the valley gently cradled by soft rolling hills. It has been more than one hundred years since the Lloyd-Jones family settled the land south of the village of Spring Green, but their legacy lives on in the buildings and ideals they left behind.

In 1864, sixty-five-year-old Richard Lloyd-Jones and his fifty-six-year-old wife, Mary, brought their five sons and five daughters to a sheltered valley forty miles west of Madison, Wisconsin. Immigrants from Wales, the Lloyd-Joneses found the terrain reminiscent of their homeland: the three contoured hills to the east, which they named Bryn Mawr, Bryn Canol, and Bryn Bach; the broad bottomland for cultivation; and the sparkling stream threading its way to the nearby Wisconsin River. As the patriarch of a close-knit family, Richard built his homestead on the low rise of a hill so that he could view the farms of his married sons and daughters adjoining his on three sides.

After Mary's death in 1870, the family celebrated her memorial at their annual Grove

Meetings, a thanksgiving for the harvest held under a bower of pines – a chapel without walls –

where sermons and hymns brought tears to the Lloyd-Jones eyes. The Grove Meetings generated

the idea of a permanent meeting place that would serve as both church and social center for the

family and their neighbors. Preparations were under way with the Chicago architect J. Lyman

Silsbee when Richard Lloyd-Jones died in December 1885. Unity Chapel was dedicated in August

1886 with a family cemetery laid out nearby.

Richard and Mary did not live to see the valley become a vibrant center for progressive

education, liberal religion, and architectural patronage. The founding of a school that introduced

a new philosophy of teaching infused with a moral purpose and set amid artistically significant

works of architecture was the contribution of Ellen and Jane Lloyd-Jones. As his two youngest

daughters did not have husbands, Richard bequeathed his land and homestead to them. Aunt Nell

and Aunt Jennie, as they were known to all, decided to create an unprecedented coeducational

venture: students would board in their home and learn in the fields and on the farm. The aunts

commissioned their twenty-year-old nephew, Frank Lloyd Wright, a fledgling architect in Chicago,

to design their building. The Hillside Home School, also known as the Home Building, was

finished in 1887.

The school grew and prospered for the next two decades and gained a national reputa-

tion. The student body, which originally consisted largely of nieces and nephews, increased in

number, drawing children from as far away as Chicago and Minneapolis. Classes were held in the schoolroom, but learning took place as often as possible in the pastures or woods nearby. Children were encouraged to identify birds and flowers while hiking or gathering berries for a pie.

Aunt Nell and Aunt Jennie expanded their vision and created a rich architectural legacy in the decade between 1895 and 1905. First they commissioned Wright to design a windmill, which was to be sited on the highest point of land behind their school. With sympathetic and indulgent clients, a commanding site, and no fixed budget, Wright produced one of his most lyrical buildings. The tower, which in plan consisted of a diamond intersecting an octagon, was one of Wright's first masterpieces – a purely utilitarian structure rendered in potent symbolic language. The windmill was completed in 1897, and Wright christened it "Romeo and Juliet" to recognize the landmark's formal and expressive dualities: masculine and feminine, function and art.

By 1901, Ellen and Jane Lloyd-Jones were ready to enlarge the school and again they turned to their nephew as their architect. The second Hillside Home School was unlike any building that had been built in the valley or anywhere in Wisconsin up to that time. The larger and more important spaces – the assembly room, laboratory, and gymnasium – were conceived as two-story volumes linked by corridors, which in one instance also housed classrooms. The wings of the school stretched out boldly into space, so that at one point the entrance road penetrated the building complex by running beneath the bridge connecting assembly room and laboratory. Yet by using a native sandstone as the dominant material, Wright integrated this revolutionary structure skillfully into its setting.

By the completion of the Hillside Home School in 1903, the population of Lloyd-Joneses in the valley had crested and begun to diminish as the second generation died off and their children left for college or moved to the city. Frank Lloyd Wright's sister Jane and her husband, Andrew T. Porter, returned to the valley in 1907, when Andrew became the school's business manager. They settled near Romeo and Juliet in a house designed by Wright – called "Tan-y-deri," Welsh for "under the oaks" – and Andrew struggled without success to resolve the school's troubled finances, which forced it to close in 1915.

Aunt Jennie died in 1917; Aunt Nell followed two years later. By that time, although few Lloyd-Joneses remained, Frank Lloyd Wright had moved to the valley and constructed his own house to the north. A former teacher, Mary Ellen Chase, described the Hillside Home School as "a school as well as a farm and a home." Many years later, Frank Lloyd Wright and his wife, Olgivanna, would revive this simple but powerful idea, infusing it with their own spirit and direction.

Unity Chapel is the only building still standing that is directly associated with Richard Lloyd-Jones. Although he never saw the building, it is the realization of his quest for religious freedom in the New World. Designed by J. Lyman Silsbee, it was constructed of wood frame and shingles in 1886. Surviving evidence suggests Frank Lloyd Wright supervised construction and may have designed details of the interior. During his lifetime, Richard's son Jenkin Lloyd-Jones, a Unitarian minister of national reputation, established a tradition of nondenominational worship by offering the pulpit to ministers and social leaders of many faiths. The chapel is maintained by Unity Chapel Inc., which consists of descendants of the Lloyd-Jones family, their spouses, and a representative of the Frank Lloyd Wright Foundation.

This photograph recorded Richard Lloyd-Jones surrounded by his descendants in 1883. The empty chair commemorates his late wife, Mary, who had died thirteen years earlier. To the right of the empty chair sits sixteen-year-old grandson Frank Lloyd Wright holding his youngest sister, Margaret Ellen, known as Maginel. To the left of Wright is his sister Jane, in the white dress, standing between their father and mother, William and Anna Wright. The two women to either side of Richard's chair are his daughters Ellen, to the left, and Jane, to the right.

The students and faculty pose for a photograph in front of the first Hillside Home School building designed by Frank Lloyd Wright. Although Wright had moved to Chicago by 1887 and opened his independent practice in Oak Park, Illinois, by 1893, he kept in close contact with the Lloyd-Jones family in the valley. In addition to serving as his aunts' architect, he sent his two eldest boys, Lloyd and John, to the school.

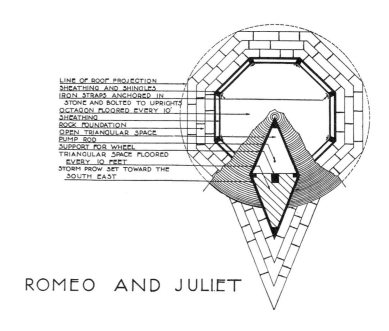

LINE OF ROOF PROJECTION
SHEATHING AND SHINGLES
IRON STRAPS ANCHORED IN
  STONE AND BOLTED TO UPRIGHTS
OCTAGON FLOORED EVERY 10'
SHEATHING
ROCK FOUNDATION
OPEN TRIANGULAR SPACE
PUMP ROD
SUPPORT FOR WHEEL
TRIANGULAR SPACE FLOORED
  EVERY 10 FEET
STORM PROW SET TOWARD THE
  SOUTH EAST

ROMEO AND JULIET

Romeo and Juliet, plan.

The slopes and woodlands were laboratory and library to the children, who were quick to identify signs of the changing seasons such as the pasque flower, the first wildflower of spring. Frank Lloyd Wright, who as a teenager had spent every summer in the valley, had also gone to school with nature. Later he remembered being drawn to the hill around which he built Taliesin because there, as a boy, he had discovered the first pasque flowers pushing their way up through the last of the March snow.

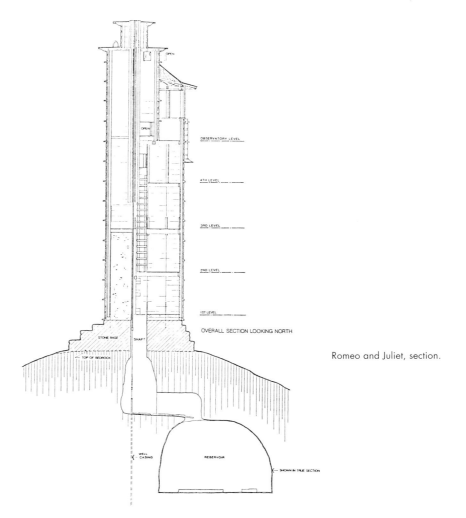

OBSERVATORY LEVEL

4TH LEVEL

3RD LEVEL

2ND LEVEL

1ST LEVEL

OVERALL SECTION LOOKING NORTH

STONE BASE   SHAFT

TOP OF BEDROCK

WELL CASING   RESERVOIR   SHOWN IN TRUE SECTION

Romeo and Juliet, section.

The patronage of Ellen and Jane Lloyd-Jones was pivotal in the early development of Wright's career as a modern architect. Their trust and determination encouraged Wright to produce his most original ideas before he presented them outside the family. The Hillside Home School was one of the first built works where Wright expressed the idea of composing the primary spaces of a public building as major masses (the gymnasium on the left and assembly room on the right) and linking them with supporting spaces (classrooms, galleries, and hall). He was soon to perfect this device in the Larkin Administration Building, Buffalo, New York (1902–6), and Unity Temple, Oak Park (1905–8); he would reinterpret it later in the Guggenheim Museum, New York (1943–59).

Aunt Nell and Aunt Jennie meant the Hillside Home School to be in part a cenotaph to their parents. Wright expressed this sentiment most clearly in the assembly room, which was intended as a sacred as well as a secular space. In addition to Sunday services at Unity Chapel, the students participated in nondenominational morning worship and vespers. The balcony, which is a square rotated forty-five degrees within the square volume of the room, is inscribed with lines from Isaiah 40, Richard Lloyd-Jones's favorite Bible verse: "Comfort ye, comfort ye my people, saith your God. They that wait upon the Lord shall renew their strength. They shall mount up with wings as eagles. They shall run and not be weary, they shall walk and not be faint."

Hillside Home School, plan.

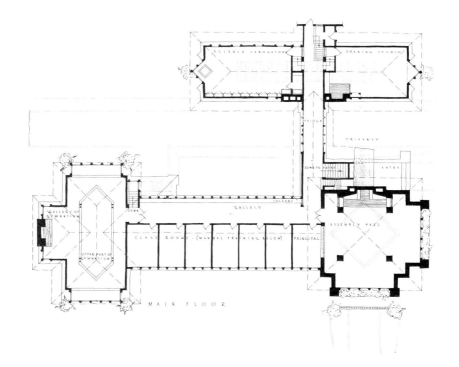

In homage to Welsh tradition, Wright used oak and sandstone obtained from the family property as the dominant building materials for the school. The fireplace mantel, like a monumental headstone for his grandparents, is engraved with a stanza from Thomas Gray's "Elegy Written in a Country Churchyard," Mary Lloyd-Jones's favorite poem, which she recited on the day she died. Wright designed the andirons as abstractions of the conical hats Richard had made and sold as a trade in Wales.

Tan-y-deri, a house built for Wright's sister Jane and her husband, Andrew T. Porter, has a square plan, a variation of his design for "A Fireproof House for $5000," published in the *Ladies' Home Journal* in April 1907. Built in the same year, Tan-y-deri was constructed of wood frame and shingles. This view shows the building carefully sited under the oak trees from which it derives its Welsh name. Today the Taliesin Fellowship owns the property, and it continues to be used as a residence.

OAK PARK HOME AND STUDIO

Frank Lloyd Wright's desire to integrate his personal and professional life began as early as 1889, when he built his first house for himself and his bride, Catherine Tobin, in Oak Park, Illinois. It was a tentative step, initially. The original building was modest, with only a living room, dining room, and kitchen on the ground floor and a master bedroom, nursery, and studio above. But as the family grew and Wright's independent practice (which he opened in 1893) flourished, additions in 1895 and 1898 made daily life more comfortable and, even more important, provided nourishment for the imagination.

The first major alteration was the addition of a second-floor playroom in 1895. Wright added a high, barrel-vaulted space where his four young children could play safely, secluded from the formal rooms. The playroom, however, also became the center of the family's social and cultural life and anticipated the playhouses, cabarets, and theaters of Taliesin and Taliesin West.

With the acquisition of a grand piano in 1905, the playroom became a music hall where the family orchestra (each child, six in all, played a different instrument or sang) performed for their own enjoyment. There were also special occasions when the children presented plays using the fireplace as a backdrop and the audience watched from a tiered gallery at the rear of the room; sometimes the arrangement was reversed, with the actors above in the gallery and the audience seated on the floor.

In 1898, with the construction of the studio, connected to the house by a passageway, Wright began to determine the future pattern of his work and life. Although Catherine and the children paid scant attention to the activities in the drafting room, the studio staff was small and intimate, and social life often flowed back and forth between the two buildings. As Wright's second eldest son, John, recalled, "Papa's parties were best of all. He had clambakes, tea parties in his studio, cotillions in the large drafting room; gay affairs about the blazing logs that snapped and crackled in the big fireplace. From week to week, month to month, our home was a round of parties. There were parties somewhere all of the time and everywhere some of the time. Bowls of apples and nuts, great jars of wildflowers were everywhere."[4]

Wright's departure from the Oak Park home and studio for Taliesin in 1911 is usually explained as the result of his failed marriage; his affair with one of his clients, Mamah Borthwick Cheney; and his desire to escape the attendant publicity that dogged him in Chicago. These certainly are the most obvious reasons. Yet it must be remembered that when Wright chose Oak Park it was a small village bordered by open countryside; he could ride his horse across the fields to the banks of the Des Plaines River. After twenty years, Oak Park was a burgeoning suburb of Chicago and the open space between Oak Park and River Forest had been replaced with single-family dwellings, many of them of his own design. It is certain that Wright felt personally and intellectually confined by Oak Park. He needed to seek an uninterrupted vista that stretched to the horizon. He had memories of just such a place, where the pasque flowers signaled the advent of spring.

The central feature of the living room, the formal space where the Wright family would entertain friends and neighbors, is the inglenook fireplace. Wright lavished attention on the details of the public rooms of his houses (the living rooms, playhouses, and drafting rooms), often treating the private rooms (the kitchens, bathrooms, and even bedrooms) as smaller, efficient service spaces. The Japanese wood-block print is evidence of Wright's early discovery of Asian art, which began while he was living in Oak Park. Wright made his first trip to Japan in 1905 in the company of his wife, Catherine, and his clients Mr. and Mrs. Ward W. Willits.

It is consistent with Wright's philosophy that after his children were born, he chose not to add more bedrooms and bathrooms but instead built a grand top-lit playroom to nourish the spirit rather than serve the body. The playroom was the antecedent of the Taliesin Playhouse and the Cabaret-Theater and Pavilion at Taliesin West. Here the Wright family, employees, and neighbors reveled in holiday celebrations, musical evenings, and, occasionally, amateur plays performed by the children. With bricks and mortar, light and space, Wright sought to feed his family's imagination. "In this room were the milestones to maturity; treasures, friends, comrades, ambitions," John Lloyd Wright testified to his father's prescience, "and through the years I have dreamed through the inspiration of this playroom."[5]

With the construction of his studio attached to his house, Wright made a decisive step from which he would never reverse himself. In 1898, five years after opening his own practice, Wright decided to unify his life and his work, if only architecturally. The studio is the first example of Wright's organization of a public building into major and minor masses (in this case, the two-story octagonal drafting room on the left and the one-story library to the right), which are joined by a circulation space (the reception hall). A passageway accessible from the drafting room leads directly to the house so that one may move between the two buildings without stepping outside.

The Oak Park drafting room was the first of five magnificent rooms Wright would design and build as studios for himself in the next sixty years. Although each one was distinctly different from the others in keeping with their varying sites in Illinois, Wisconsin, and Arizona, they all shared certain elements: diffused or indirect light; spatial exuberance; and the strategic placement of works of art (in this case, the frieze he designed for the Heller House, Chicago, 1897) as sources of inspiration.

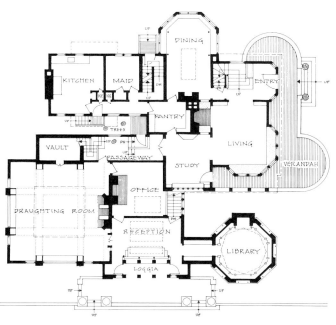

Wright's private office, where he received clients and contractors, is located directly off the reception hall. A door opening to the main drafting room allowed him ease of access to supervise and consult on plans. The chairs and cabinetry were designed by Wright, who after 1900 increasingly sought to unify his buildings and fur-nishings. The house and studio were both richly appointed with three types of decorative art, which would reappear at Taliesin and Taliesin West: Asian (pri-marily Japanese and Chinese), Native American, and objects of Wright's own design (such as the weed holder, ca. 1895, placed prominently on the desk).

Oak Park Home and Studio, plan.

T A L I E S I N

To Fashion Worlds in Little

Making Form

As God Does One with Spirit

So God Makes Use of Poets

To Fare on, Fusing

The Self that Wakes

And the Self that Dreams

We Find for Choosing

The Deeds to Dare

And the Laws to Keep

Adapted in 1912 by Frank Lloyd Wright
from Richard Hovey, *The Masque of Taliesin*

Taliesin – a house, an architectural studio, a farm, a school, a life of music, art, dance, and design – can best be understood as a manifestation of the aesthetic and cultural ideals of Frank Lloyd Wright. Wright's most personal composition is the consummate example of the architectural self-portrait. In its landscape, gardens, buildings, art, and furnishings, Taliesin embodies his frontier spirit and his cosmopolitan tastes, both characteristics of his intricate intelligence and his romantic idealism.

Taliesin was built in 1911, when Wright left his family and closed his practice in Oak Park to take up residence with Mamah Borthwick (who reassumed her maiden name after her divorce) in the valley settled by his grandparents. The choice of the low and projecting hilltop, known from his childhood, allowed him an uninterrupted 135-degree panorama taking in all the former family sites and the cluster of buildings of his own design at the Hillside Home School. Following in the Lloyd-Jones tradition, Wright chose a Welsh name for his property, condensing many meanings with one word. Taliesin was a Welsh bard or poet celebrated in myth and literature; but literally the word means "shining brow," a phrase that Wright used to describe the way the house wrapped around the slope of the hill. With one poetic stroke, the creator became identified with the creation; henceforth, Taliesin was Wright's alter ego.

From the beginning, he envisioned Taliesin as part of the agrarian ideal, complete with farm buildings, orchards, gardens, and broad drives. "I saw it all, and planted it all," he wrote, "and laid the foundation of the herd, flocks, stable and fowl as I laid the foundation of the house."[6] His love of and dedication to the farm life of his Lloyd-Jones forebears must be set beside the obvious pleasures of city life that he had discovered during his years in Chicago. Above all, the integration of his architectural studio and his house, initiated in Oak Park, defined life at Taliesin. It was a life increasingly set against a backdrop of Asian art – particularly Japanese woodblock prints, screens, and textiles – and surrounded by books and music.

Little is known of the details of Wright's daily life with Mamah Borthwick at Taliesin between 1911 and 1914. Since Wright's first wife, Catherine, refused to grant him a divorce, the social stigma attached to their circumstances distanced them from their neighbors. Nevertheless, Wright had created an idyllic world, which was soon to come to a swift and violent end. The residential wing of Taliesin and his life with Mamah Borthwick were both destroyed on August 15, 1914, when a servant set fire to the building and killed Mamah, her two children, and four employees. Left only with the explanation that the servant had gone mad, Wright was shattered. Many years later, he wrote, "After the first terrible anguish, a kind of black despair seemed to paralyze my imagination in her direction and numbed my sensibilities. The blow was too severe. I got no relief in any faith nor yet any in hope. Except repulsion, I could feel now only in terms of rebuilding. I could get relief only by looking forward toward rebuilding – get relief from a kind of continuous nausea, by work."[7]

The second Taliesin was begun almost immediately on the foundations of the first. Although to speak of Taliesin I, II, and III is to acknowledge the destruction of the residential wing in two fires (another occurred in 1925 as the result of faulty wiring), it is more accurate to say that Taliesin was never finished. Year in and year out until his death in 1959, Wright's energetic spirit was forever motivating him to knock out walls, rebuild terraces, and rearrange furniture and art.

Taliesin II is associated with Wright's extended absences from the United States, beginning in 1916 while he designed and supervised construction of the Imperial Hotel in Tokyo. During his prolonged stays, which lasted until 1922, Wright indulged his passion for art collecting. Taliesin accommodated his wide-ranging interest in Asian art in the organization of interior details: Japanese screens were integrated into walls, woodblock prints were framed in wood stands, pillows and tables were covered in antique embroidered silks. Dione Neutra, who accompanied her husband, Richard, during a stay at Taliesin in late 1924, wrote that "there were magnificently painted screens in gold and silver on which were painted either colored flowers or clouds with birds or dark green fir boughs." She concluded, "This estate is like a fairyland."[8]

Dione Neutra, newly arrived from Europe, was deeply impressed with Taliesin, which was both an architectural office and a house built to serve Wright's employees and a flow of guests that included his grown children, friends, and clients. She came too late, however, to meet the most constant visitor at Taliesin between 1915 and early 1924, Wright's companion, Miriam Noel. Wright had met her shortly after the tragic events of 1914, and they began living together almost immediately. Still unable to obtain a divorce, he spent almost ten years with Miriam in uncertainty and turmoil. In 1922, Wright was granted a divorce from Catherine, and a year later, at the filing of the final decree, he and Miriam were married, but she left for good only a few months later.

In the summer of 1924, after a building campaign of five years in Japan and a year in Los Angeles trying to establish a practice and revive his finances, Wright returned to Taliesin. Despite these absences, he was forthright about his preference for the stability of a permanent home over the temptation of travel. "Dust settled on the heads of the ancient gods at rest upon the broad ledges," he confessed. "But Taliesin had been calling me all these years and I was looking forward to the time when it should come alive again for me and all those I loved."[9]

The buildings and grounds of Taliesin had unquestionably suffered during Wright's six years in Japan and California. The second fire, in 1925, provided an opportunity to alter and enlarge the house once more. It was a building program that would continue with some interruptions over the next thirty-four years, twenty-one of which he would spend in Arizona during the winters.

Earlier that year, Wright had fallen in love with Olga Lazovich Hinzenberg, a twenty-six-year-old native of Montenegro whom he had met in Chicago late in 1924. Their plans to marry were postponed until August 1928 while Miriam Noel Wright launched a barrage of legal and financial maneuvers that ultimately forced Wright to leave Taliesin, created such chaos that the local bank stepped in and took title to the property, and resulted in auctions that disposed not only of the art (that which escaped the 1925 fire) but of farm machinery and Wright's personal possessions as well. Finally, in September 1928, after the desperation of the situation peaked, a small group of Wright's staunchest supporters financed the return of the property by purchasing shares in Wright Inc., a venture founded on the future earning potential of the architect.

Upon his return to Taliesin, Frank Lloyd Wright, accompanied by his wife, Olgivanna, their three-year-old daughter, Iovanna, and Svetlana, Mrs. Wright's eleven-year-old daughter by her first marriage, found the damp rooms virtually empty, with remains of furniture and books scattered about in disarray. Slowly, however, Wright began repairs to reverse the neglect and damage that had occurred after he lost ownership of Taliesin.

Circumstances only worsened after the stock market crash of 1929; but at the same time, seeds of hope were sown as Wright and Olgivanna began to discuss starting a school. "We've got everything but money," he confided to his eldest son, Lloyd. "I guess there is none anywhere except in the savings banks or hidden in socks or under the cellar-floor."[10] They sent out a formal announcement about the opening of the school, and in October 1932, the first apprentices arrived at Taliesin. A proposed institutional framework never materialized; Wright preferred his "learning by doing" method, which would take place in the drafting room, on construction sites, and on the farm. Wright recalled, "As the plan of the Taliesin Fellowship unfolded itself, I had hoped that apprentices – like the fingers on my hands – would increase not only my own interest and enthusiasm for my work as an architect, but would also widen my capacity to apply it in the field."[11]

The founding of the Taliesin Fellowship in 1932 was the impetus for the renovation and remodeling of the Hillside Home School, which had fallen into disrepair after its closing more than fifteen years earlier. Plans proceeded for the conversion of the gymnasium into a playhouse for weekend entertainment of music and films, the assembly room into a Fellowship living room, and former classrooms into a dining room. At about the same time, Wright designed a larger drafting room to be added behind the original building. Within a few years, this room was a flurry of activity as Wright's practice revived with commissions for houses, such as Fallingwater for Edgar Kaufmann in Mill Run, Pennsylvania (1934–37), and public buildings, such as the Johnson Wax Administration Building in Racine, Wisconsin (1936–39).

After the years of privation and disrepair, by the middle 1930s, Taliesin regained its poetic serenity. When future apprentice Curtis Besinger visited in 1939, he found "a simple life being lived with a seemingly small income and yet with luxurious abundance." He noted that "fresh produce came from the vegetable garden, eggs from the henhouse, milk and butter from Midway [the farm buildings]. . . . Contained within that Wisconsin Valley. . . were the vineyard, the orchard, the pastures dotted with cows, and the various fields devoted to crops such as hay, corn, and oats."[12]

In the winter of 1937, while the buildings at Taliesin and Hillside were under reconstruction, Wright purchased land in Arizona to build a new Taliesin. It is paradoxical that the tranquility Wright was intent on creating was most often broken by himself. As his son John observed, "He was a series of surprises; was expert in getting himself in tight positions, delighted in being confronted with difficulties. . . . One day he remarked, 'Things seem to be going along too smoothly – things are too quiet.' To curtail his momentum made him uneasy. But his anxiety was always unfounded for the quiet never lasted. . . . Like a river, he was incessant, unexhausted."[13]

The dining area, ca.1912, with built-in cabinetry and furniture by the architect. Wright framed a Japanese woodblock print – a pillar print, so named because they were intended for display in the house, mounted on a pillar – in a stand of his own design.

Through several rebuildings, the garden courtyard view of Taliesin remained faithful to the original organization of 1911. This photograph was taken by Henry Fuermann, who provided an accurate record of Taliesin I with 8 x 10 glass negatives. The house, visible at the right, is separated from the studio, at the left, by a loggia that opens to a vista of the Wisconsin River. When he left suburbia for good, Wright drew on myth and metaphor to transform and transcend his work of the Oak Park studio. Wright explained, "Taliesin was to be an abstract combination of stone and wood, as they naturally met in the aspect of the hills around about." To create a potent symbolic language, he used "stone stratified... in the lower house walls and up from the ground itself into the broad chimneys. This native stone prepared the way for the lighter plastered construction of the upper wood-walls.... And the lines of the hills were the lines of the roofs, the slopes of the hills their slopes, the plastered surfaces of the light wood-walls, set back into shade beneath broad eaves, were like the flat stretches of sand in the river below and the same color, for that is where the material that covered them came from."[14]

This very rare view of the living room of Taliesin I may date to as early as 1912. The composition – three individual photographs presented as a triptych in the style of Japanese prints – leads to speculation that Frank Lloyd Wright, an amateur photographer, may have taken it.

The sublime relationship between buildings and landscape is evident in this view of Taliesin II, ca. 1915–17. The original entrance led the visitor along a broad drive that completely encircled the house, visible on the slope above. The road began a gentle ascent into the garden courtyard; on arriving, the visitor would be directly on axis with the loggia, which framed a view of the Wisconsin River beyond. Hills, fields, river, and woods – the Wisconsin native had elevated these local elements to a composition of universal dimensions.

The living room is dominated by the massive fireplace built of limestone laid in horizontal ledges and capped by an enormous block of stone. From the built-in seat the visitor would face a bank of windows that frame a panoramic view of the stream and pond, the Welsh hills, and Unity Chapel. Wright surrounded himself with books, music, and art in every form, whether ceramic, bronze, or textile. During her stay in 1924, Dione Neutra and a small group of others played Bach and Handel here. The living room left her almost speechless. "It is so many-sided and different," she remarked, "but more beautiful than anything I have ever seen before."[15]

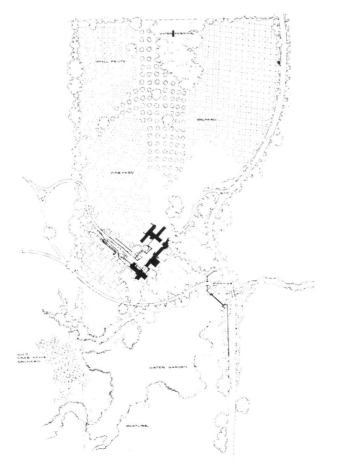

Taliesin I, plot plan.

In the studio, Wright displayed art and the tools of the architect – his drawings, models, and drafting equipment. Two unbuilt commissions appear in models, the San Francisco Press Building (1912), to the right, and the Abraham Lincoln Center, Chicago (1902), to the left. Resting on the mantel are three hanging scrolls remounted as panels, *Descent of the Amida Trinity and Attendant Bodhisattvas* (see page 143); to the left, a Buddhist figure and a Buddhist head (see page 144).

Taliesin II was richly ornamented, "a feast for the eyes," as Wright often remarked. In the loggia, a room created in the rebuilding after 1914, the contrasting textures and colors of Asian art added depth and resonance to the interior. Japanese screens, Chinese pottery, Buddhist figures, a Chinese carpet on the floor, Japanese textiles over the table and used as upholstery were probably acquired by Wright on one of his five trips to Japan between 1916 and 1922. Tragically, most of this collection was destroyed in the fire of 1925.

The flow of guests through Taliesin — whether staying only for a few hours or for months — has never diminished. Wright was a gregarious and charming host; he entertained Sherwood Anderson, Charles Lindbergh, Philip Johnson, Anaïs Nin, Charles Laughton, Alexander Woollcott, Clare Booth Luce, Erich Mendelsohn, and Ludwig Mies van der Rohe as well as hundreds of other friends, neighbors, clients, and family members in Wisconsin and Arizona. Carl Sandburg knew Wright for decades but visited infrequently. In the mid-1920s, Wright and Sandburg were photographed on the grounds of Taliesin in Wisconsin.

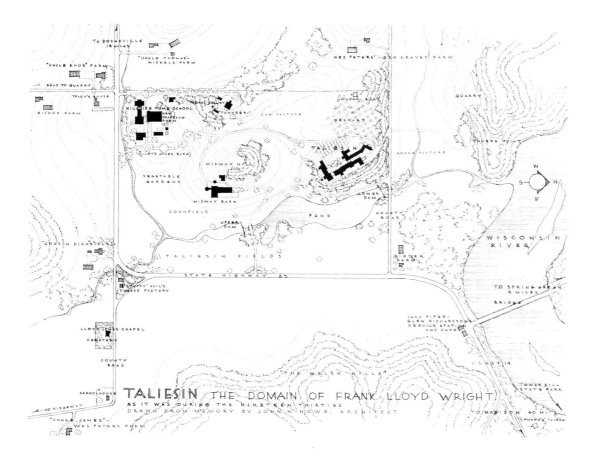

By the late 1930s, Wright owned all the land between Taliesin and Hillside. He moved the entrance to Taliesin to the east, adjacent to a second dam, which had been constructed below Midway Barns. This plan also indicates the location of the former Lloyd-Jones farms: that of Wright's grandfather Richard (Hillside Home School), surrounded by those of his sons, Thomas (to the west), Enos (to the southwest), John (Cousin Dick's, to the southeast), and James (directly east). The service station, located near the banks of the Wisconsin River, was eventually purchased by Wright, who designed a restaurant, Riverview, for that site. Today it serves as the Frank Lloyd Wright Visitor Center.

During the Depression years, it was not only educational but essential that Taliesin be operated as a working farm. Former apprentice Curtis Besinger recalled, "all of the Fellowship was involved, with varying degrees of acceptance and pleasure, in work on the farm and in the garden.... There," he explained, "we had a large vegetable garden, a flock of chickens that provided fresh eggs and occasionally meat, and a herd of dairy cows providing fresh milk twice a day as well as cream for butter and sour milk for cottage cheese."[16]

The tradition of a formal evening of dinner and music dates from the earliest days of the Taliesin Fellowship. On Sundays, the meal was served in the living room, followed by a concert: Haydn, Mozart, or Brahms might be played by the quartet, the chorus would perform, and then a piano solo might end the evening. This view shows Wright and his wife, Olgivanna, with their daughter, Iovanna, seated on the floor, and Svetlana, Mrs. Wright's daughter, to her left, playing the violin.

Wright, Olgivanna, and Iovanna on a Sunday afternoon picnic in the Wisconsin countryside with the Taliesin Fellowship, ca. 1940.

Wright sketching in the field with apprentices near Midway Barns, 1950s.

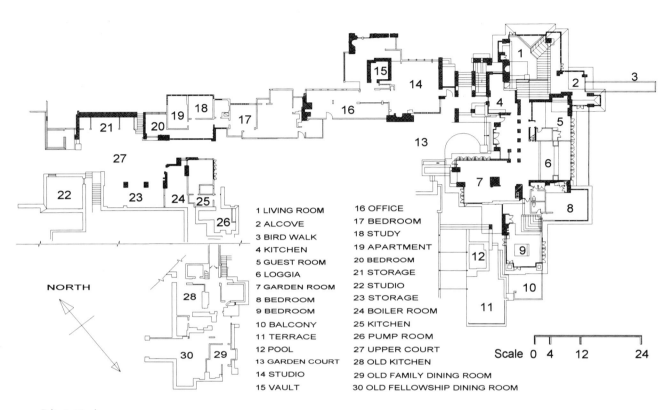

1 LIVING ROOM
2 ALCOVE
3 BIRD WALK
4 KITCHEN
5 GUEST ROOM
6 LOGGIA
7 GARDEN ROOM
8 BEDROOM
9 BEDROOM
10 BALCONY
11 TERRACE
12 POOL
13 GARDEN COURT
14 STUDIO
15 VAULT

16 OFFICE
17 BEDROOM
18 STUDY
19 APARTMENT
20 BEDROOM
21 STORAGE
22 STUDIO
23 STORAGE
24 BOILER ROOM
25 KITCHEN
26 PUMP ROOM
27 UPPER COURT
28 OLD KITCHEN
29 OLD FAMILY DINING ROOM
30 OLD FELLOWSHIP DINING ROOM

NORTH

Scale 0 4   12   24

Taliesin III, plan.

The landscape at Taliesin is given equal weight with the architecture; the setting and the buildings complement each other. There are three zones of plant material and garden features at Taliesin: the flower gardens in the interior courtyard; a transitional zone of shrubs and trees around the perimeter of the building; and the fields and pastures of the farm. One of the most picturesque elements is the spring-fed stream that meanders through the valley until it joins the Wisconsin River to the north. In 1911, Wright built a dam across the stream at the entrance to the property. In so doing, he created a pond, which made the water visible from the house above, and a waterfall, which marks the visitor's arrival at Taliesin. The sound and sight of the tumbling water, the foam, and the spray create a dynamic rather than static garden ornament and serve as a powerful metaphor for the juxtaposition of the man-made and natural worlds.

The entrance to Taliesin from the automobile courtyard, with the house to the left and the studio at right. The limestone steps and retaining walls reinforce the poetic idea that the building grows out of its site.

The wings of the house, on the right, and the studio, on the left, wrap around the garden courtyard in an intimate embrace. Wright's skillful siting of Taliesin around its hilltop created two distinct experiences: the prospect and uninterrupted vistas of the surrounding countryside gained from within the house, and the sense of enclosure and protection found inside the courtyards. The manicured lawn and flower gardens where the plant world is tamed and within easy reach reinforce the feeling of direct contact with nature.

The dining area, while spatially a part of the living room, maintains its own presence by the contrast between the Japanese screen and the Wright-designed furnishings. The proportions and dimensions of the rear wall were calculated to accommodate a sixfold Japanese screen painting, such as the *Kitano Shrine Compound, Kyoto* shown here (see pages 140–41). In the late 1930s, the circular chairs (a version of a chair originally designed around 1904 for the Darwin D. Martin House, but modified in the late 1930s for the Herbert Johnson House) were added.

The Taliesin Fellowship, which includes the Frank Lloyd Wright School of Architecture and Taliesin Architects, is in residence in Wisconsin from late spring until the onset of autumn. The living room at Taliesin is the focal point for many of the social events and receptions held throughout the summer. After the 1925 fire, Wright redesigned the living room and loggia, extending the height of the ceilings and adding a balcony and second-floor bedrooms. Materials used on the exterior of the

building – limestone, warm sand-colored plaster, and wood trim – are repeated in the interior. Numerous Buddhist figures are visible throughout the room: the cast-iron Chinese sculpture, Quan Yin, in the middleground; to the left, a stone head of the Cosmic Buddha; the standing Amida Buddha, a Japanese wood figure, on the balcony; and directly to the right of the Amida Buddha, a ceramic head built into the limestone wall; the last piece, no doubt, a fragment saved from the 1925 fire.

The guest bedroom is enlivened by spatial complexity, light entering from the sides and from above, and the fine stonework of the limestone wall and fireplace. A fragment from the 1925 fire, a Chinese stone figure of Quan Yin, is built into the mantel to the left of the fireplace opening.

One of the most dramatic and mysterious spaces in the house is the loggia that flows into the garden room, an interior created by enclosing the former porte-cochere. A freestanding fireplace, open on three sides, defines the edge of the garden room. The art and furnishings contribute to the power of the loggia: a sixfold Japanese screen dating from the Momoyama period (late sixteenth to early seventeenth century), *Pine, Blossoming Cherry, and Camelia* in ink, color, and gold leaf on paper by an anonymous Kano school artist; a rare Chinese wool carpet; and a Japanese wood figure of the Amida Buddha on the balcony. Several decorative objects from Wright's Oak Park period can also be seen, right to left: a pair of art-glass doors and an iridescent wall sconce (on the ceiling shelf) from the William R. Heath House, Buffalo (1905); and a weed holder, ca. 1895, on the table.

Frank Lloyd Wright's bedroom terminates the long hall that begins in the living room. It faces southeast and commands a 135-degree view, off the balcony, of Unity Chapel and the family graveyard, and Romeo and Juliet above the Hillside Home School. Wright frequently enlarged and remodeled this room throughout the years, each time extending it farther and farther into the garden.

The studio, although untouched by the fires that twice destroyed the house, was in a constant state of remodeling by Wright during his lifetime. In the 1930s, after the drafting room at Hillside was built, the studio continued to be used as Wright's office. Today the Taliesin Fellowship occasionally uses this room for small meetings. Important works of art, from right to left, include a seated Amida Buddha in wood and lacquer, a Chinese stone relief panel of a Bodhisattva mounted on the pier, and a portrait of the architect's mother, Anna, above the fireplace. Below the stone relief is a chair from the Oak Park studio, and to the left, a dining table and chairs from the Usonian House installed in *Sixty Years of Living Architecture,* a 1953 exhibition at the Guggenheim Museum, New York.

Eventually Wright added larger farm
buildings, locating them near a hill
halfway between Taliesin and Hillside.
Thus, they are called Midway Barns.
They were used most actively during the
mid-1950s, when the Taliesin Fellowship had sole operation of the farm.

The Hillside Playhouse was the location of formal Saturday evenings, which included dinner and performances of instrumental and choral music by the Taliesin Fellowship, until it was consumed by fire in 1952. Frank Lloyd Wright, seated at the piano in the music pit, is seen rehearsing with a string quartet; a corner of the stage is visible at the left.

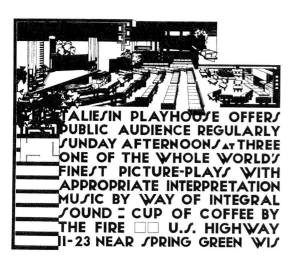

TALIE/IN PLAYHOU/E OFFER/
PUBLIC AUDIENCE REGULARLY
/UNDAY AFTERNOON/ AT THREE
ONE OF THE WHOLE WORLD'/
FINE/T PICTURE-PLAY/ WITH
APPROPRIATE INTERPRETATION
MU/IC BY WAY OF INTEGRAL
/OUND □ CUP OF COFFEE BY
THE FIRE □□ U.J. HIGHWAY
11-23 NEAR /PRING GREEN WI/

The renovation of the Hillside Home School for the Taliesin Fellowship began with Wright's design for a room in which to project movies and hold musical and theatrical performances. The Playhouse was created by remodeling the former gymnasium of the boarding school. From its opening on November 1, 1933, until the declaration of war in 1941, the Playhouse was open to the public on Sunday afternoons, when mostly foreign films by directors such as René Clair or Sergei Eisenstein were shown. "During that first year the programs did not stop because of the winter weather," an apprentice explained, "and before the steam heating system was installed tremendous fires were kept going in the fireplace all night long."[17]

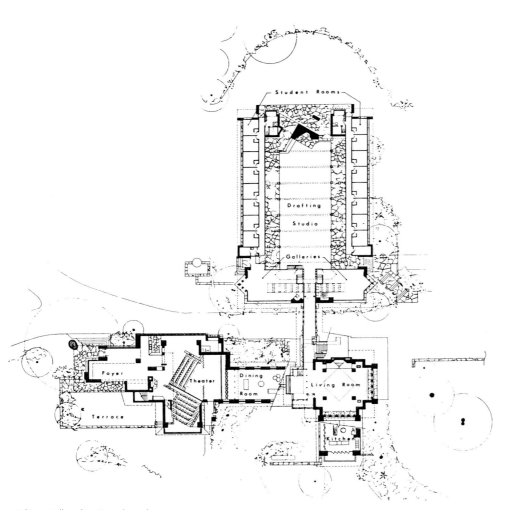

Student Rooms

Drafting

Studio

Galleries

Foyer

Theater

Dining
Room

Living Room

Terrace

Kitchen

Taliesin Fellowship Complex, plan.

In 1952, one half of the former Hillside Home School was destroyed by fire, but the Taliesin Fellowship living room, behind the two trees to the right, was untouched. This unforeseen event gave Wright the opportunity to redesign the dining room and theater without the limitations imposed by an existing building. On the exterior, the major change consisted of reducing the height of the theater.

The Taliesin Fellowship Complex consists of the former Hillside Home School
and a new wing (containing the drafting studio and dormitory rooms) added
in 1933–38. The original materials –
sandstone, wood frame, and plaster –
were also used in the later addition,
the low structure at the right.

The Fellowship takes most meals in the dining room, which dates from 1952–54. The spatial flow through the three major rooms – the living room, dining room, and theater – is uninterrupted and steps down in tiers. This photograph shows the view from the balcony off the living room with the theater visible beyond, through movable pierced screens. The tables are set for a formal evening, a tradition at Taliesin since the inception of the Fellowship in the 1930s. The black-tie event begins with cocktails, followed by dinner, and usually culminates with music in the theater. Sometimes these occasions celebrate a special occasion, such as Frank Lloyd Wright's birthday, June 8.

In his autobiography, Wright wrote of his mother's belief in a healthy diet, and her insistence on the natural flavors of fruit, vegetables, and whole grains. Speaking of himself, Wright recalled, "for the first twelve years of life he got a ginger-cookie now and then...but 'store candies' only when mother didn't know it. No pie. No cake – except at other houses as he grew older."[18] On his birthday he indulged his sweet tooth with a cake that combined all the confections that he had been forbidden early in life.

Birthday Cake

Separate 70 eggs, mix and beat the yolks well (with a spoon) with 10 cups sugar till lemon colored and foamy. Add 10 cups flour. Beat egg whites till very stiff and fold in. Butter and flour bread pans. Bake three-quarters to one hour in 300° oven. Take out, cut across in two to make layers. Makes 16 bread pans and one cake pan. Inner filling: Nuts, strawberry jelly, and whipped cream. After filling has been placed between the layers, cut cake in slices and top with frosting. Chocolate frosting: Melt together 4 tablespoons butter, 6 cups sugar, 24 squares chocolate, 6 cups water. Top with whipped cream.[19]

As redesigned, the theater featured an innovative seating plan that was noted by critic Aline B. Saarinen, who saw it shortly after its completion in 1954. She explained that Wright's new ideas consisted of "the audience sitting on two sides of a 90-degree angle so everyone gets a three-quarter view of the performance: a wood floor with space beneath to act as a virtual drum-head, intended to give resonance without reverberation."[20] The magnificent stage curtain (see pages 132–34) was designed by Wright and made by the Taliesin Fellowship.

The roof of the drafting studio is supported by a series of eight wood trusses that create an angular rhythm across the room – Wright called it "an abstract forest." Light enters through clerestory windows from two sides and above. The daily work of the Frank Lloyd Wright School of Architecture and Taliesin Architects is carried on here.

A massive sandstone fireplace stands at the northern end of the drafting studio. Two objects from an early Wright building, the Midway Gardens, Chicago (1913–14), are visible at the right: a concrete relief panel and *Sprite,* a poured concrete sculpture.

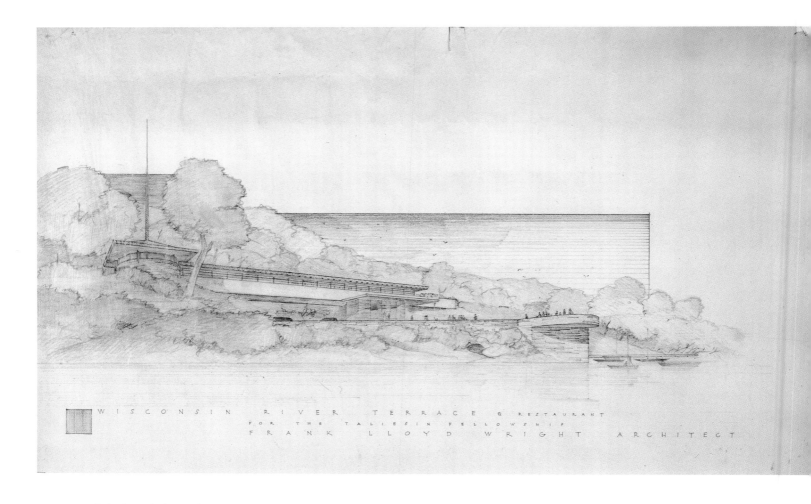

WISCONSIN RIVER TERRACE & RESTAURANT
FOR THE TALIESIN FELLOWSHIP
FRANK LLOYD WRIGHT ARCHITECT

In 1953, Frank Lloyd Wright designed a restaurant for the property at the entrance to the valley where Taliesin is located. As the building echoed in its overall form the nearby bridge that spans the Wisconsin River, Wright called it "Riverview." Not completed until after the architect's death, it served for many years as a restaurant and now has been converted to the Frank Lloyd Wright Visitor Center.

"I wanted a home where icicles by invitation might beautify the eaves. So there were no gutters," Wright admitted. "And when the snow piled deep on the roofs and lay drifted in the courts, icicles came to hang staccato from the eaves. Prismatic crystal pendants sometimes six feet long, glittered between the landscape and the eyes inside."[21]

TALIESIN WEST

And thou, America,

Thou too surroundest all,

Embracing, carrying, welcoming all, thou too

By pathways broad and new, approach the ideal.

The measured faiths of other lands,

The grandeurs of the past, are not for thee,

But grandeurs of thine own,

Deific faiths and amplitudes, absorbing, comprehending all,

All in all to all.

Give me, O God, to sing that thought,

Give me, give him or her I love this quenchless faith, in this,

Whatever else withheld withhold not from us,

Belief in plan of thee enclosed in time and space.

Condensed by Frank Lloyd Wright from Walt Whitman's "Song of the Universal,"
Leaves of Grass, engraved on a red concrete slab at the entrance to Taliesin West

In December 1937, Frank Lloyd Wright purchased a plot of Sonoran desert at the base of the McDowell Mountains twenty-six miles northeast of Phoenix, Arizona. For most of his seventy years – beginning with his earliest childhood memories and continuing with life at Taliesin – Wright had been rooted to the green hills of Wisconsin. "Living in the Desert is the spiritual cathartic a great many people need," he explained. "I am one of them." The Fellowship was five years old and established; his practice and national reputation were rebounding; and after years of tragedy and neglect, both Taliesin and Hillside were undergoing active rebuilding. It was just this settled existence that Wright's restless intellect abhorred. "Fed up with too sweet Midwest pastoral domesticity, I began taking the desert....The spiritual cathartic that was the desert worked – swept the spirit clean of stagnant ways and habitual forms ready for fresh adventure. As that fresh adventure, for one thing, I designed the camp which we began to build."[22]

The building of Taliesin when Wright was forty-four years old was the inevitable return of the prodigal son to his homeland; but the building of Taliesin West was the act of a man of seventy seeking a rebirth. Unlike the word "Taliesin," which Wright chose for its symbolic associations, it was simply a coincidence that the name of his new hometown, Phoenix, was identified with the bird of Egyptian mythology that, consumed by fire, rose from its own ashes.

The aftermath of the 1925 fire had been only one of Wright's problems in January 1928, when he was first summoned to Arizona by a former draftsman to consult on the building of a new hotel, the Arizona Biltmore. Legal and financial entanglements resulting from his divorce from Miriam Noel Wright took him to the brink of personal and professional ruin. But just as the bank was taking possession of Taliesin, he was finalizing the details of a commission that would bring him back to Phoenix in February 1929. On his return, he built his first camp, Ocatilla, to house his draftsmen while they prepared the working drawings for San Marcos in the Desert, a new resort near Chandler, Arizona. Although the stock market crash of 1929 put an end to all construction plans, Wright's experience at Ocatilla made an indelible impression. "I presently found that the white luminous canvas overhead and canvas used instead of window glass afforded such agreeable diffusion of light within, was so enjoyable and sympathetic to the desert, that I now felt more than ever oppressed by the thought of the opaque solid overhead of the much too heavy mid-western house."[23]

Wright, along with his family and the Taliesin Fellowship, returned twice, for the winters of 1935 and 1936, before acquiring acreage on a low rise that afforded views of the village of Scottsdale in the distance. With the building of Taliesin around a projecting hilltop, Wright was following the family precedent set by his grandfather and the architectural precedent set by Thomas Jefferson at Monticello; but with the bold decision to venture out across the desert floor, Wright was a genuine trailblazer. There is no record that he ever had second thoughts. "That desert camp belonged to the desert," he stated, "as though it had stood there for centuries."[24]

While Taliesin had been built, at least partly, on the life of the farm, Taliesin West was based on the life of the Taliesin Fellowship. Above all, the camp was the center of a way of life dedicated to architecture deriving its inspiration from raw nature and the restorative powers of art and music. Beginning in 1938, the Fellowship made annual migrations to Arizona, leaving

Wisconsin usually after Halloween and returning sometime after Easter. As a result, construction proceeded slowly over three winters, with excavation and roadwork undertaken in 1938; the drafting room, kitchen, dining room, apartments, Wright's office, and a room, known as the Kiva (a masonry cube titled after the half-submerged underground chamber of the Pueblo Indians), for dining and the projection of films, built in 1939; and quarters for the Wright family and accommodations for the apprentices erected in 1940. Interiors were in the finishing stages early in 1941, just months before the United States entered World War II.

The buildings are neither large nor monumental, but they command a presence on the landscape. The low walls of boulders and concrete seem an extension of the desert floor, and the angular forms overhead (redwood and canvas, originally) call to mind the tents of a nomadic tribe. Unlike Taliesin, which is one building coiling itself around the pinnacle of a hill, Taliesin West was designed as movement through a cluster of pavilions that simultaneously outline and juxtapose themselves against the nearby and distant mountains. Philip Johnson has observed that "at Taliesin West, Frank Lloyd Wright made the most intriguingly complex series of turns, twists, low tunnels, surprise views, framed landscapes, that human imagination could achieve."[25] "My friends," Johnson declared, "that is the essence of architecture."[26]

Work on the camp slowed and then came to a standstill during the war years; but by the late 1940s, the returning GIs and arrivals from Europe and Asia swelled the Fellowship to double its former size. The major alteration at Taliesin West was the addition of a larger playhouse, called the Cabaret-Theater, built in the winters of 1950 and 1951, replacing the Kiva, which became a library. Music, art, and, after 1932, films played a central role in the life of Taliesin. The Cabaret-Theater was the location of the weekend's relaxation; there, formal dinners were held with music and a movie following. Curtis Besinger, a former apprentice, recalled that "Mr. Wright was a movie fan; he enjoyed good films. But he saw the great movies of the world as something more than entertainment; he saw them as a form of education in the deepest meaning of the word. They were not only a means of acquiring information about the various cultures of the world, but of nourishing and developing one's own creative resources. They were like the works of art which he acquired and with which he surrounded himself and the Fellowship. They were, as he often said, his library."[27]

Alterations, additions, and improvements continued at Taliesin West as they did at Taliesin. "Thanks to our seasonal migrations," Besinger pointed out, "Mr. Wright was able to view Taliesin and Taliesin West with a fresh eye each time he arrived at one of them."[28] For the remainder of his life, as the Fellowship began to spend longer periods of the year in Arizona, Wright experimented with the light framework of the buildings by redesigning and replacing the wood beams and canvas, then by substituting sheets of glass for some canvas panels, and eventually, completely enclosing certain areas with glass. Some of the changes were to correct problems such as roof leaks, others in response to the needs of a larger Fellowship, but Wright's energetic imagination never considered Taliesin or Taliesin West complete. As former apprentice Marya Lilien remarked after Wright outlined future changes at Taliesin West, "What amazed me was here, before me, was a man of 77 planning on what he was certain he would be doing when he reached 87. He was, in fact, anxiously looking forward to it."[29]

As the postwar building boom picked up through the 1950s, Wright, who was busier than ever, prospered. This healthy financial picture enabled him to plan and undertake continuous construction at both Taliesin and Taliesin West. To accommodate the growing Taliesin Fellowship and provide facilities for music and dance performances that were staged annually, construction of a larger theater, called the Pavilion, was begun in 1954.

Bearing in mind Wright's habit of remodeling both Taliesin and Taliesin West, it would be easy to assume that he viewed them primarily as "laboratories," where he experimented with forms and spatial ideas before presenting them to clients. The danger of this viewpoint is that it denies the complex artistry, history, and symbolism that establish both properties as two of the most important landmarks of American architecture. This interpretation would also reduce Wright to what his son John described as "the architect who merely reproduces facts of life without adding to our compensation of it – without supporting it by all the weight of his spiritual experience – love, tenderness, joy."[30] Both Taliesin and Taliesin West reveal, more than any of his other buildings, a closer understanding of Wright the man as well as Wright the architect. They stand as his autobiography in wood and stone.

Between January and March 1929, Wright and a few draftsmen built walls of boards and battens and roofs and openings of canvas stretched on wood frames, the gables painted a deep red. The cabins, which encircled a central campfire like a wagon train, were sited on a low mound south of Phoenix at the base of the South Mountains (formerly the Salt River Mountains). Wright called the compound "Ocatilla," after a native cactus with tall slender stalks that give forth a scarlet flower.

Ocatilla was a temporary camp, meant to last no longer than the season or two Wright intended to spend building the resort hotel San Marcos in the Desert. While there, he reveled in the spectacular location, taking great delight in having breakfast in "that wonderful dining room sixty miles wide, as long and tall as the universe."[31] In this view, Wright's eldest son, Lloyd, is seated at the piano in March 1929.

By 1940, the first phase of construction at Taliesin West – office, drafting room, kitchen, dining room, apartments, and the Kiva (a small theater for dining, music, and films) – was substantially complete. The massive desert masonry walls, which seemed to emerge from the site itself, contrast with the light redwood framework and stretched canvas – like a tent set up on nature's own foundation. This view shows the western end of the drafting room, on the right, and the office, a detached building, on the left. Before the war, Wright landscaped Taliesin West with native cacti such as prickly pear (in the massive planter, center), cholla, staghorn, and saguaro (at the far left).

The drafting room viewed from the eastern corner of the office, 1940.

In 1940, the drafting room, with a model of the ill-fated San Marcos in the Desert in the foreground, was roofed with stretched canvas hung between redwood beams. Light entered from two sides, from high above on the north, and low to the horizon on the south. At seventy-two, Wright was more than twice the age of the apprentices who worked at the drafting tables.

Frank Lloyd Wright, at the drafting table, giving a talk to members of the Fellowship in the breezeway in spring 1946. From left to right: Kay Davison, Kenn Lockhart, Ted Bower, John Howe, Peter Berndtson, William Wesley Peters, Svetlana Wright Peters, and Cornelia Brierly.

Wright responded to the Sonoran desert with a new form of construction called "desert masonry." This technique called for gathering nearby rocks and placing them in wood forms, with flat stones facing out, and boulders in the center for fill. Concrete was poured into the forms, filling the gaps between the rocks; when dry, the forms were removed, creating a massive wall expressive of the texture and color of the surrounding desert floor.

Wright's earliest plans for Taliesin West called for a Fellowship dining room located east of the drafting room opposite the kitchen. Since this room faced south to southwest, it was built with enclosing desert masonry walls on three sides that stopped short of the overhanging flat roof. The walls and roof protected the interior from the penetrating rays of the sun, with horizontal and vertical slots providing views out to the sky and distant mountain peaks.

East of the kitchen and directly behind the apartments was the breezeway, which connected the studio and residential wings. This view, ca. 1946, looks toward the corner of the Kiva, in the middle distance. As the Fellowship grew larger in the 1950s, this area was enclosed with glass and became the dining room.

To the east of the dining room was a compact residential wing that housed apartments, one for William Wesley Peters and his wife, Svetlana (Mrs. Wright's daughter, who had married Peters in 1935), and one for another apprentice, Eugene Masselink. This view reveals how Wright transformed such common and inexpensive building materials as rock and concrete into sublime form: deep voids puncture the solid block while a play of light across the wall face contrasts with horizontal shadow lines impressed on the surface. The imprint of the shallow V-shaped channels was said to have been inspired by the striations Wright observed on the walls of a nearby canyon.

By 1940, residential quarters for Wright and his wife, Olgivanna, were ready for use. The L-shaped plan contained a living room – called the Garden Room – in one wing, for private use and Fellowship events; and bedrooms and a sitting room in the other wing. At the hinge of the L were located kitchen, bath, and an intimate room with a large fireplace, called the Cove. The two wings enclosed and opened onto a walled oasis with a small plunge pool, the one area of green garden at Taliesin West. This view, taken in about 1946, looks diagonally across the lawn from the bedroom wing into the Garden Room.

Taliesin West expresses the dualities of tent and cave; it is both open and closed. In the Garden Room, seen here ca. 1946, the rear wall, with flaps for air circulation, is solid, affording privacy; while opposite, the room opens directly onto the green garden. The roof is insubstantial, with the stretched canvas providing diffused light throughout the room.

During Wright's lifetime, Taliesin West was completely surrounded by desert wilderness, miles and miles of nothing but saguaro, cholla, and staghorn cactus. He remembered that when he first saw the site, he drove "up to a great mesa in the mountains. On the mesa just below McDowell Peak we stopped, turned, and looked around. The top of the world!"[32] This shot, taken in around 1950–54 from Maricopa Hill, just to the east of Taliesin West, shows the studio and house with apprentice quarters in the center; a house, called Sun Cottage, for the Wrights' daughter, Iovanna, to the left; and the office and Cabaret-Theater to the right. Scattered throughout the desert (visible to the right) are tents, designed and constructed by apprentices as their own dwellings. In the distance are the Phoenix Mountains and Squaw Peak.

Frank and Olgivanna Lloyd Wright at
Taliesin West in the 1950s.

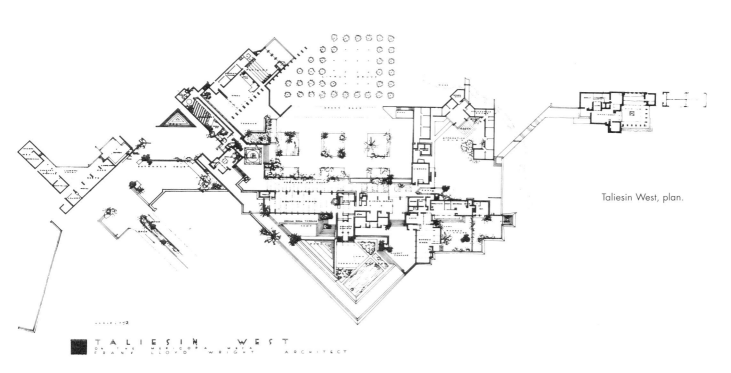

Taliesin West, plan.

TALIESIN WEST
ON THE MARICOPA MESA
FRANK LLOYD WRIGHT ARCHITECT

Frank Lloyd Wright's office greets the visitor at the entrance. In the 1950s, Wright built the Cabaret-Theater and then the Pavilion (seen at the right in the background) to the east. Today the office serves as a reception room.

The desert masonry walls rise high in Wright's office, with windows located discreetly to capture views to the north, toward the McDowell Mountains, and east, toward Maricopa Hill. As Taliesin West stood for many years in the desert, the original materials used overhead – redwood and canvas – proved unsatisfactory for a permanent building. The intense heat of the summers, which can average between 110 and 115 degrees, blistered the wood and weakened the fabric. The constant replacement of these materials was impractical, and finally the wood trusses were reinforced with steel, painted Cherokee red, and plastic was substituted for the canvas.

The drafting room is located at the western end of the east-west axis, which cuts through the plan of Taliesin West as a pergola and walkway connecting the working and living spaces of the compound. At the far right is the drafting room vault, the first section of Taliesin West to be built. Originally designed to store drawings, it houses today the plotter for all the drafting room computer stations. Computers are used extensively in the work of the Taliesin Architects and by the apprentices in the Frank Lloyd Wright School of Architecture.

Fellowship life has always adhered to a schedule, with set times for rising, dining, work, and music practice. The communal bell, located between the drafting room and dining room, is rung to announce the beginning of meals. Apprentices, who live far out in the desert in tents or shelters of their own design and construction, view the sunrise as they walk to breakfast at 6:30 A.M.

The Fellowship maintains supplies and cooks in quantities that impress visitors to the kitchen. Dozens of loaves of bread are baked each week in addition to the numerous pastries, pies, and cakes that are served at breakfast, lunch, and dinner. The kitchen, just off the drafting room, is accessible on three sides. It is a meeting place to pick up a cup of coffee or read messages on a communal bulletin board.

The daily brown bread – a nutritious staple of stone-ground wheat – is a traditional Taliesin recipe that links Frank Lloyd Wright to his mother and the Lloyd-Jones family. Wright's uncle John operated a mill beside the stream in Wisconsin and produced stone-ground flour for all the Lloyd-Jones households. The bread sits on a plate Wright designed for the Imperial Hotel, Tokyo (1913–22).

The Fellowship and their guests take most of their meals in the dining room, a space that was created by enclosing an outdoor area with glass. The chairs are based on a design Wright made for the Midway Gardens, Chicago (1913–14); they were fabricated by Kenn Lockhart in the 1960s for use at Taliesin West. The breezeway, beyond the glass doors, is on the center line of the north-south axis of the compound. When seen from the pergola, the loggia becomes a dimly lit cavern through which to view the desert floor falling away to the south; when we look north from the Sunset Terrace, this open space directs our eye toward Thompson Peak, rising above the building.

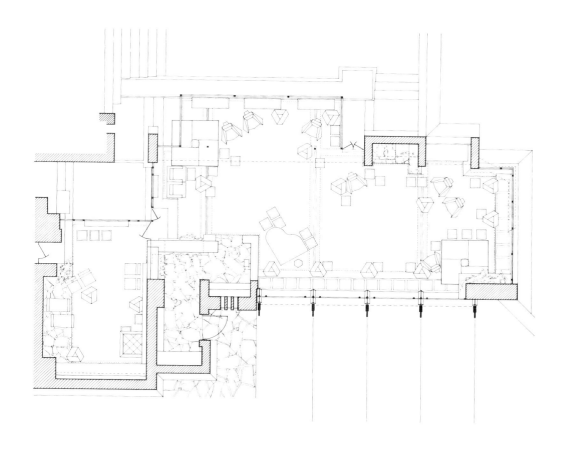

Garden Room, plan.

The Garden Room has undergone
many remodelings since its construction
in 1940. A massive fireplace has been
built at the southern end, fixed glass
clerestories have been added to provide views of the mountaintops, and
the room has been completely enclosed
by glass so it can be mechanically
heated and cooled for year-round use.
The room is designed to accommodate
a variety of Fellowship events, from
large gatherings, such as a cocktail
party for seventy-five people during
the formal evening, to conversations
beside the fireplace for only two or
three. The lounge chairs, which were
added in the early 1950s (see page
130), complement the angularity of the
architecture.

In order to provide a room where the Fellowship could sit down to dinner and then view a film, Wright designed and built the Cabaret-Theater, between 1949 and 1951. The long rectangular space was carved out of the desert floor and then covered with a flat roof.

With solid walls on three sides and flaps that close on the eastern face, it is ideal for watching movies. Cabaret tables for four to six are placed in front of long benches, while at the rear of the room one large table accommodates special guests.

Dinner is usually followed by the Fellowship and their guests' adjourning to the nearby Pavilion for music. On formal evenings, the chorus and the chamber music group perform here. The Pavilion is also the site of holiday celebrations; this photograph shows the room decorated and the tables set for Christmas dinner.

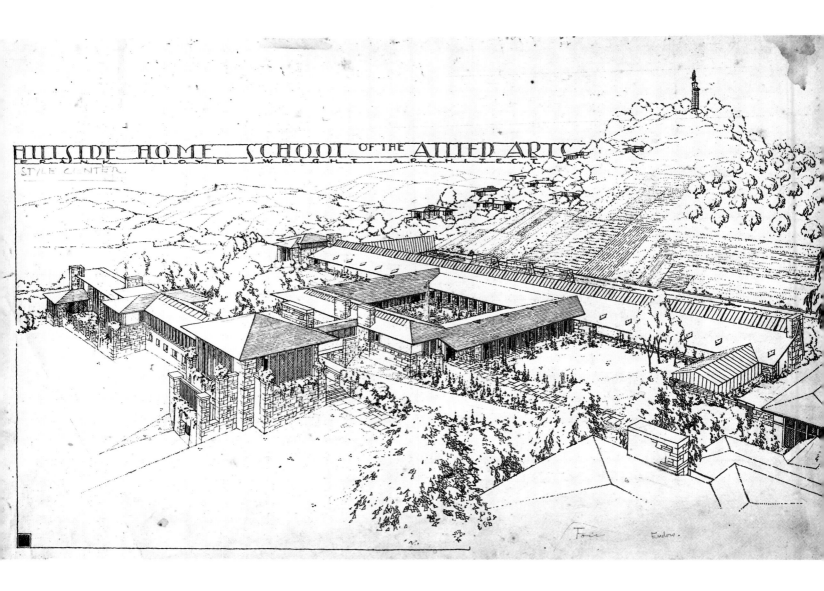

HILLSIDE HOME SCHOOL OF THE ALLIED ARTS
FRANK LLOYD WRIGHT ARCHITECT
STYLE CENTER.

W O R K

Work, whether in the drafting room, in the kitchen, or on the farm, has always been an integral part of Taliesin life. As a boy, Frank Lloyd Wright had toiled in the Lloyd-Jones fields "adding tired to tired," as he often declared. "Work *was* adventure," Wright remembered thinking, "when you were fit for it."[33]

From the beginning, Taliesin has been an architectural studio. In addition to producing plans and drawings, executing models and specifications, and overseeing construction, apprentices develop skills in a remarkable variety of occupations, including carpentry, masonry, planting and harvesting, cooking and baking, playing an instrument or singing, sculpture, graphic design, and printing.

During the Depression, Taliesin was virtually self-sufficient, with most of the Fellowship's

food produced on the farm. Tenant farmers managed the livestock and planted the fields, but

apprentices aided in the farmwork. John Howe, who joined the Fellowship in 1932, recalled those

early years in this way: "All work was considered creative, none merely menial, with everyone

participating in maintenance, whether as cooks or kitchen helpers, firing the boilers or turning out

the lights, cleaning the chicken house or milking the cows. In summer a garden period occurred

during the hour after early breakfast, with all wielding hoes against a hopeless onslaught of

weeds....[Mr. Wright] personally directed all work whether it was at the quarry, lime kiln, sawmill,

threshing operations, corn shucking, or the multitude of construction and reconstruction projects

that were continually in progress. No project was ever 'finished'; all was in a state of constant

change. Change was sought and embraced, stagnation abhorred."[34]

In addition to construction and engineering, the Fellowship developed skills in cabinetry,

carpentry, weaving, upholstery, and sewing to produce the furnishings for Taliesin and Taliesin West.

Some of the projects were small, such as cabinets or desks for apprentice rooms, designed and

made by the occupant; others were ambitious group efforts, such as the fabrication of a stage cur-

tain, completed in 1956, for the Hillside Theater (see pages 81, 132–34).

For several years, before the founding of the Taliesin Fellowship, Wright and his wife,

Olgivanna, had been formulating plans for a school. As early as 1928, they proposed a program

called the Hillside Home School of the Allied Arts, an architectural program with instruction in

the form of workshops devoted to pottery, glasswork, metalwork, painting, sculpture, dance, and drama. The prospectus was published in 1931 under the title "Why We Want This School"; but

within months, the Wrights had rejected an academic model in favor of an apprenticeship system.

One project Wright planned from the outset of the Fellowship was the publication of a magazine

that would expose the apprentices to, among other things, graphic design and typography. Although

the magazine never produced more than a few issues, it was followed by the publication of a

broadside, *A Taliesin Square-Paper,* which was issued periodically between 1941 and 1953.

It is interesting to note that as the Taliesin Fellowship evolved over the years, it ventured

into many of the allied arts originally proposed. Between 1950 and 1970, apprentices learned

dance as well as other aspects of the theater – set design, costume design, and lighting – when

dance classes evolved into the Taliesin Festival of Music and Dance and a series of dance dramas

written and choreographed by the Wrights' daughter, Iovanna.

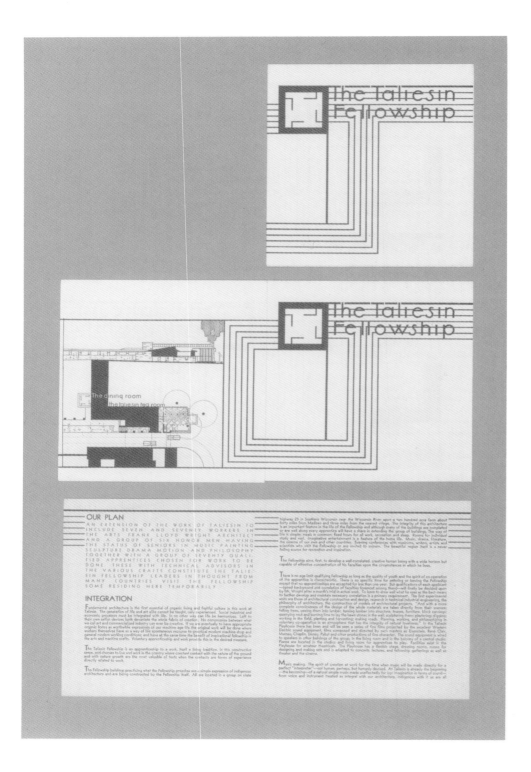

Graphic design, typography, and fine printing had been an interest, even an avocation, of Frank Lloyd Wright's dating back to Oak Park. With the founding of the Taliesin Fellowship, Wright launched a venture, known informally as the Taliesin Press, working closely with his apprentice Eugene Masselink. Through the years, the Taliesin Fellowship has edited, designed, and printed a variety of publications, including pamphlets, broadsides, theater programs, and cards. This pamphlet was published in December 1933; it describes the Taliesin Fellowship and includes an application form. The cover illustrates the Hillside Playhouse, which was open to the general public for movies and light refreshments.

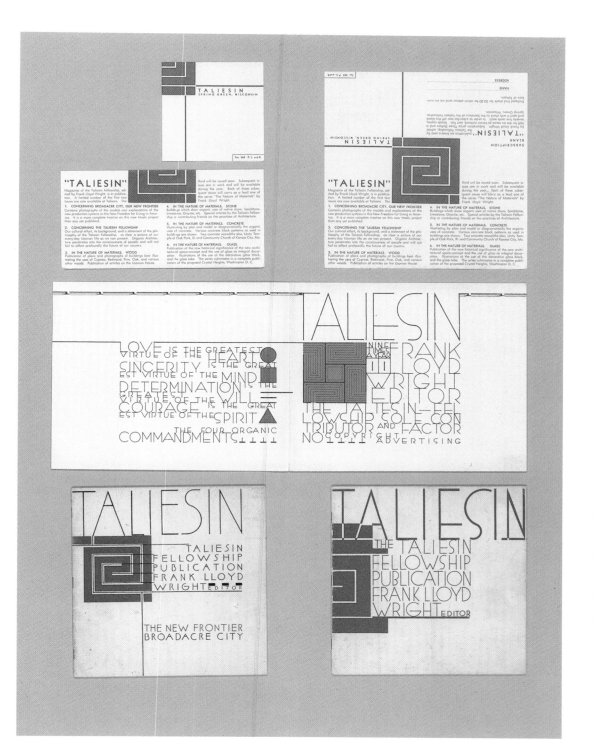

From the inception of the Fellowship, Wright announced a publication program that would have as a corollary purpose experiments in typography and fine printing. The first of these publications was a magazine, *Taliesin*, which was to appear nine times a year. Only one issue, in a rectangular format, was produced, in 1934. The idea was revived in 1940 with a less ambitious schedule of six times a year. However, only two issues, in a square format, were published; the first, October 1940, devoted to Broadacre City (a project incorporating Wright's urban planning principles), and the second, February 1941, on the Taliesin Fellowship. The subscription blank is a particularly fine example of Wright's graphic design ideas; the square format is repeated in the insignia of the Taliesin Fellowship, which unifies all four quadrants of the sheet when it is folded twice into a self-mailer.

The magazine was superseded by a broadside, *A Taliesin Square-Paper, A Nonpolitical Voice from Our Democratic Minority,* which first appeared in January 1941. This publication was printed on newsprint and when folded twice assumed a square format. It appeared intermittently during World War II and occasionally thereafter until 1953.

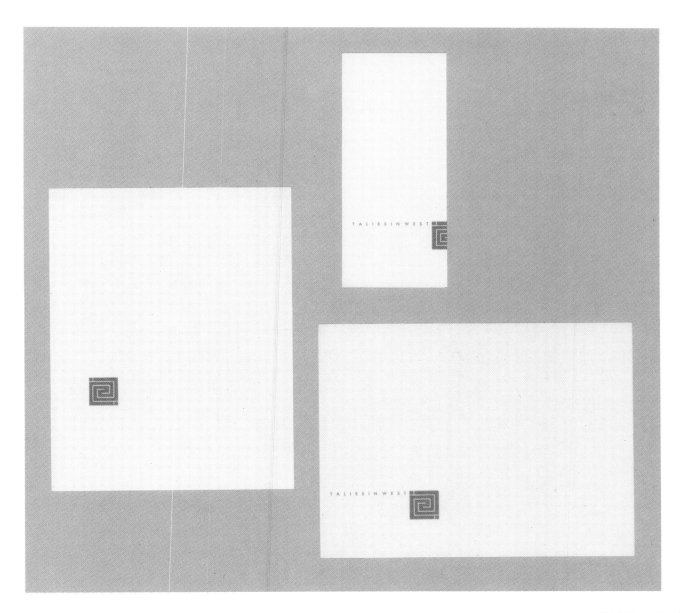

This Taliesin West letterhead, designed
by Eugene Masselink in the early 1950s,
is representative of Taliesin graphic
design. The paper is a standard size,
8 ½ x 11 in., but the original design
is achieved through the placement of
the insignia and the orientation and
folds of the sheet.

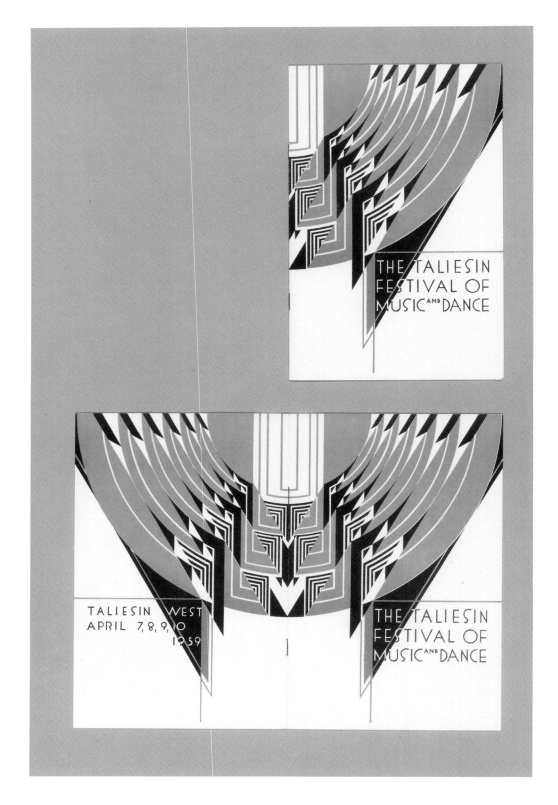

The Taliesin Festival of Music and Dance was inaugurated in the Pavilion at Taliesin West in April 1957 and held annually thereafter through April 1970. Many of the programs were designed by Eugene Masselink, who was responsible for most of the graphic design at Taliesin from the 1940s until his death in 1962.

Music was always a part of life at Taliesin, and it continues to play an important role for the Fellowship. "Each of us was encouraged to play a musical instrument or sing in the chorus (or both)," John Howe recalled, "so, following dinner, we performed for Mr. and Mrs. Wright and their guests, as well as for ourselves. In our chapel services we sang music by Palestrina and this continued to dominate our programs for many years. Also the words to Bach's 'Jesu, Joy of Man's Desiring,' were changed to 'Joy in work is man's desiring,' and this was our Fellowship 'hymn.'"[35] The design of this music stand dates from the mid-1940s. One stand is in the living room at Taliesin and another in the theater at Hillside.

A majority of the furniture at Taliesin and Taliesin West is either built-in or made at Taliesin to complement the architecture. This chair dates from Taliesin II (1914–25) and is constructed from pine, machine-cut, with details such as the wide top rail and flat arms that accentuate the grain of the wood. The loose cushion rests on the seat, which cantilevers slightly forward.

This lounge chair, sometimes referred to as the "origami" chair because its planes appear to be folded, was added to the Garden Room in the early 1950s. The design dates from 1946–49.

The practice of the fine arts of painting and sculpture as they relate to architecture can be traced through the history of the Taliesin Fellowship. The work of Eugene Masselink went beyond graphic design to include abstractions. This tempera on paper, *Flowering Cactus*, 25⅜ x 19⅞ in., was painted in 1951 and is typical of Masselink's interest in depicting underlying geometric forms found in nature.

Overleaf:
One of the largest textile works undertaken at Taliesin was the fabrication of a theater curtain in 1956 as a replacement for one that was destroyed by fire. The design by Frank Lloyd Wright is an abstraction of the countryside that surrounds Taliesin – the green hills, plowed fields, and red barns. His signature red square appears at the lower right.

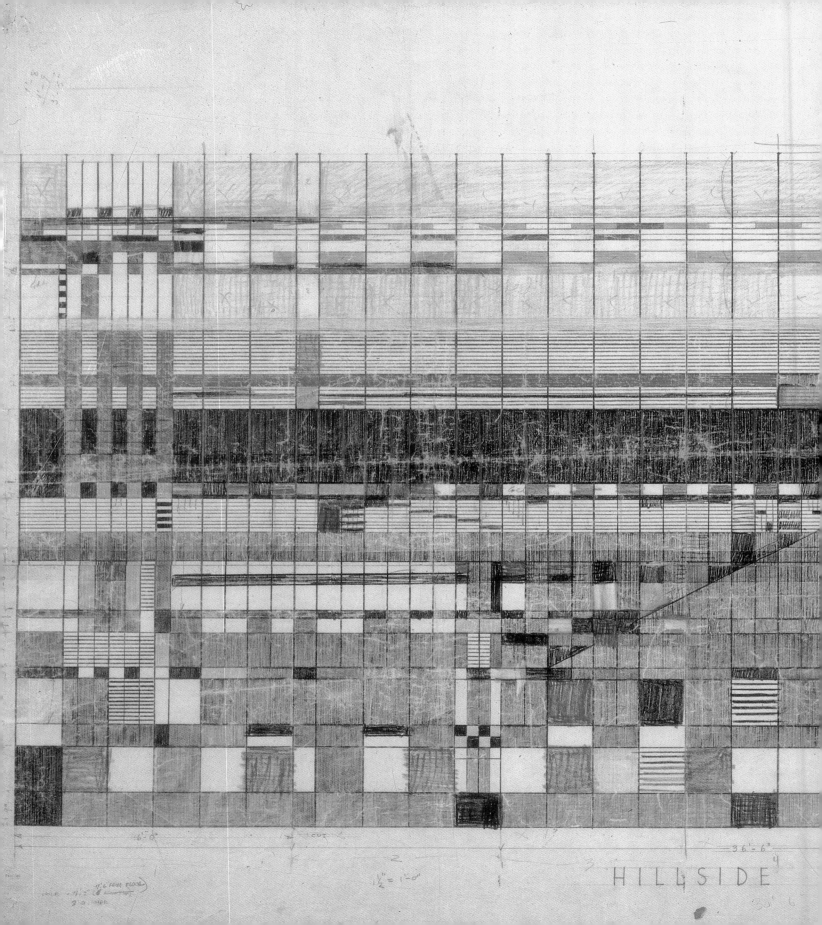

HILLSIDE

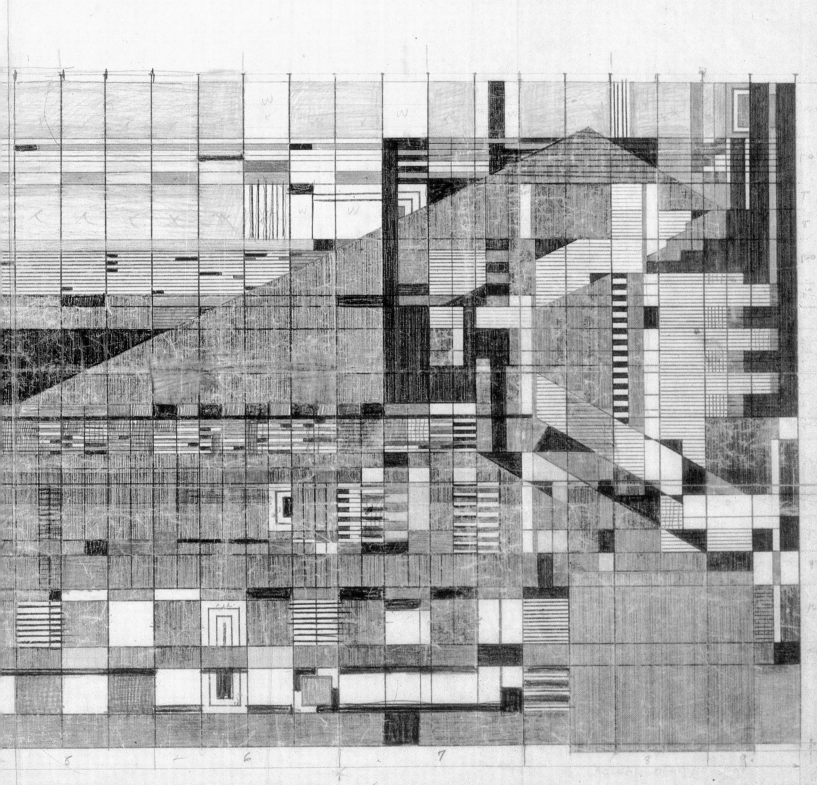

ATRE CURTAIN

This detail of the theater curtain reveals the materials of which it is made: off-white cotton canvas as background; squares and rectangles of red, black, yellow, brown, and green felt and gold synthetic lamé; cotton yarn; and gold cord. The felt patches are affixed only at the corners to increase flexibility when the curtain is drawn back.

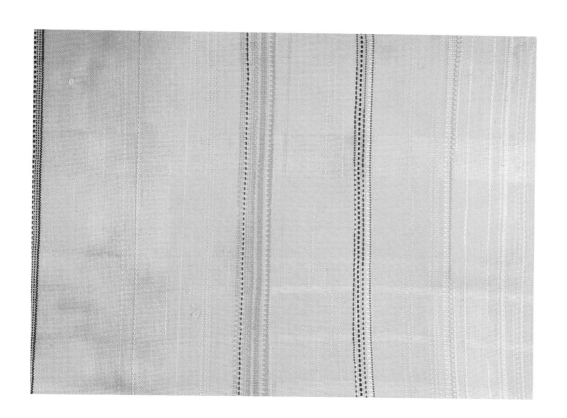

For the most part, textiles used for upholstery and floor covering at Taliesin are purchased; however, there were periods when an active interest was taken in weaving. In 1941, under the direction of the textile designer Henning Watterston, looms were installed on the balcony adjacent to the Hillside living room. Later, in about 1948, at Taliesin West, looms were again set up. This photograph shows a detail of a fringed shawl, 86 x 34 in., woven by Olgivanna Lloyd Wright in 1948 using wool yarn.

Apprentice Lois Davidson is shown here at the loom set up outdoors at Taliesin West in 1948. Photographs of the Garden Room taken in the 1950s show some of these weavings draped over the back of a chair or across a tabletop.

A   R   T

Frank Lloyd Wright's philosophy of domestic design was summarized by his son John as a belief "that an instinct for the beautiful would be firmly established by a room whose simple beauty and strength are daily factors."[36] The art, architecture, and furnishings of Taliesin and Taliesin West are not merely a shell for, but an expression of, the life that unfolds within. Every detail – whether a stanza of a poem inscribed on a plaque, a piece of Chinese porcelain sitting on a shelf, or an exquisite Japanese screen incorporated into the wall – contributes to that life and the education of all within.

The young architect's first home in Oak Park was full of decorative objects. Before the turn of the century, Wright exhibited a preference for plaster copies of Classical sculpture, such as the *Venus de Milo* and the *Winged Victory;* but he soon discovered Asian art, especially Japanese woodblock prints – *ukiyo-e* – by artists such as Hiroshige, Hokusai, and Utamaro. His collection of these works as well as ceramics, lacquerware, Chinese rugs, and Japanese screens would only increase after a trip to Japan in 1905.

Totoya Hokkei. *Earth,* from the series
The Five Elements of the Suikoden.
Color woodblock, 8 ⅜ x 7 ⅛ in.

It is clear from his description of Taliesin I that Wright designed it with his collection of Asian art in mind. He wrote, "As work and sojourn overseas continued, Chinese pottery and sculpture and Momoyama screens overflowed into the rooms where, in a few years, every single object used for decorative accent became an 'antique' of rare quality."[37] So few photographs of the interiors of Taliesin I have survived that it is impossible to reconstruct those rooms with accuracy.

However, Taliesin II, which is associated with Wright's numerous trips to Japan between 1916 and 1922 during the building of the Imperial Hotel, became a virtual museum of Asian art. Wright's fascination with Japanese prints in particular puts him in the company of the Impressionist and Post-Impressionist painters, including the Europeans Claude Monet, Paul Gauguin, and Henri de Toulouse-Lautrec and the Americans Mary Cassatt and James McNeill Whistler. It is well known that in the late nineteenth century these artists acquired woodblock prints and that the Japanese aesthetic influenced the development of modern art. Yet even Monet's collection at Giverny did not equal the sheer quantity and splendor of the screens, scrolls, porcelains, textiles such as fragments of priests' robes or whole garments such as *kosode* (short-sleeved robes), Japanese prints, and Buddhist sculpture that covered almost every surface of Taliesin II.

The destruction of this immense collection of art in the fire of 1925 was a tragedy surpassed only by the lives lost in the fire of 1914. In contemplating the scorched shards, Wright vowed, "they should live on in me . . . . I would prove their life by mine in what I did."[38] As proof, he "picked from the debris partly calcined marble heads of the Tang dynasty, fragments of the black basalt of a splendid Wei-stone, soft-clay Sung sculpture, and gorgeous Ming pottery that had turned to the color of bronze by the intensity of the fire." He fulfilled a promise to "put the fragments aside to weave them into the masonry fabric of Taliesin III."[39]

By 1930, Wright's collection was further decimated by bank repossessions and auctions precipitated by his divorce from Miriam Noel Wright. But with the revival of his fortunes in the 1940s and 1950s, he began to acquire new objects for both Taliesin and Taliesin West. The collection today can be divided into two categories: art that is integrated into the architecture or displayed in the interiors and gardens in Wisconsin and Arizona, and objects that are kept in museum-quality storage.

Whether inside the buildings or outside on the grounds, the art collection is thought of as a library providing inspiration, instruction, and nourishment for the intellect and the imagination. The prints, textiles, and screens collected in various periods in Wright's life – some even surviving from his travels in Japan – constitute an essential feature of the architectural self-portrait that is Taliesin and Taliesin West.

"Antique or modern sculpture, paintings, pottery, might well enough become objectives in the architectural scheme," Wright wrote, "and I accepted them, aimed at them often but assimilated them . . . . as integral features."[40] The dimensions and proportions of certain walls of Taliesin – especially in the dining alcove, loggia, and studio – were clearly built to receive sixfold

Japanese screens. This view shows the *Kitano Shrine Compound, Kyoto,* a six-panel screen, 34 ¾ x 87 ⅜ in., painted in ink, color, and gold leaf on paper in the first half of the seventeenth century (Edo period). This genre painting, currently mounted in the living room behind the dining room table, portrays springtime visitors to a famous Shinto shrine in northwest Kyoto.

This six-panel screen, *Pine Tree with Pheasants and Ducks,* in ink, color, and gold leaf on paper, 60½ x 140¼ in., was painted by an anonymous Kano school artist in the eighteenth or nineteenth century (Edo period). It depicts flowers and birds associated with spring and summer and was intended to be paired with another screen representing autumn and winter. Photographs of Wright's studio dating from the late 1920s show this screen mounted high on the east wall.

From the beginning, the studio at Taliesin, which was spared in the fires, contained a vault where Wright stored and conserved works on paper and fragile textiles. These two paintings on paper, *Lovers with Attendant* (left) and *Woman Playing Samisen and Woman Writing Letter* (right), possibly part of a larger composition, are attributed to Iwasa Matabei or the school of Matabei. They were painted in the early seventeenth century in ink, silver leaf, gold powder, and gold leaf, and each measures 51½ x 22¼ in.

After 1914, Wright placed *Descent of the Amida Trinity and Attendant Bodhisattvas*, 52 ¾ x 47 ⅞ in., in a prominent position over the studio fireplace (see page 58). This triptych of hanging scrolls (remounted as panels) is painted in ink, color, and gold pigment on paper and dates from ca.1728 (Edo period). The theme derives from Pure Land Buddhism: the descent (*raigo*) of the Amida Buddha and a host of heavenly beings who come to welcome the soul of a departed to paradise.

Wright, who is recognized as a connoisseur of Japanese art, understood that during the Edo period there had been no distinctions between what is regarded in the West as fine art (painting and sculpture) and crafts (textiles, ceramics, and so on). Japanese garments such as *kosode* (short-sleeved robes) were produced with the same attention to detail and often with the same elaboration of a theme as a six-panel screen. During his various stays in Japan between 1916 and 1922, Wright purchased quantities of fine textiles in the form of complete garments as well as pieces of garments. This example, three joined fragments of *ramie* (bast fiber) from a *katabira* (an unlined summer *kosode*), dating from the early eighteenth century, measures 32 ¼ x 54 ½ in. The workmanship exhibited in the embroidery, stencil pattern imitating tie-dye, and ink underdrawing is exquisite; depicted is a branch of a flowering cherry tree with an interlocking pattern of stylized tortoise shells with cherry blossom centers.

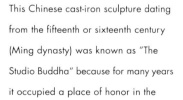

This Chinese cast-iron sculpture dating from the fifteenth or sixteenth century (Ming dynasty) was known as "The Studio Buddha" because for many years it occupied a place of honor in the drafting room (see page 58) at Taliesin. It appears in photographs dating as early as the 1920s along with other Buddhist art Wright kept over the fireplace.

This *katsugi* (a *kimono*-shaped head covering worn by an upper-class woman outdoors) superbly illustrates Wright's affinity for Japanese design. The garment, dating from the nineteenth century, is constructed from a gauze-weave silk with stenciled and stitch-resist tie-dye and measures 54 ½ x 51 in.

Wright's major interest in Asian art, verging on an obsession during the height of his acquisitions in Tokyo between 1916 and 1922, was the pursuit of the Japanese color woodblock print. On his return to Taliesin, Wright reserved a special place of honor in the vault for his favorite printmaker, Andō Hiroshige. *Niijuku Ferry,* number 93 from Hiroshige's landscape series, *One Hundred Famous Views of Edo,* dates from 1857 and measures 13 ¾ x 8 ⅞ in. Of this series, Wright declared, "a new thing under the sun came with it, through Hiroshige – a breadth and bigness of treatment that insist upon a sense of the whole scene of which the view shown is but a glimpse in detail."[41]

Wright had a particularly fine eye for *surimono*, privately printed, limited-edition color woodblock prints. *Surimono* resulted from a collaboration between poet and artist, both of whom sought to portray elements of daily life by allusion to classical literature, drama, and myth. The thirty-one-syllable poems, *kyōka*, which appear in the margins, convey complex meaning using puns, literary references, and nature symbolism. *A Parody of Kajiwara no Kagesue* by Katsukawa Shuntei, dated ca. 1818, represents the legendary warrior Kagesue as a contemporary beauty. Intended as a New Year's card, this *surimono* measures 8⅜ x 7⅜ in.

The Japanese prints were kept in the vault at Taliesin, but Wright brought them out to share with the Fellowship for "print parties." The evening began with a *sukiyaki* dinner prepared on *hibachis* on the terrace off of his bedroom and was followed by a discussion indoors of the art and craft of *ukiyo-e* and *surimono* as Wright held up individual prints for examination.

This *surimono*, *The Empress Kōmyō*, 8½ x 7½ in., from the series *Three Beauties*, by Ryūryūkyo Shinsai, dates to ca. 1820.

As a connoisseur of Japanese prints, Wright was extremely knowledgeable about printing techniques. At the print parties, he would often explain the process of making handmade paper and the use of delicate inks and opulent materials such as metallic powders and pigments, including mother-of-pearl. This color woodcut, *Ushiwakamaru Defeats Benkei in a Game of Sugoroku*, by Totoya Hokkei is printed with a brass background and uses other metals in the details. Dating from around 1825, it measures 8¼ x 7¼ in.

舞雲雀
声も
高根と
丈さろらへ

桂花

熨斗目ほと
霞む裾野や
春さき不二

二橋

Along with Hiroshige, Frank Lloyd Wright ranked Katsushika Hokusai as one of the world's supreme artists, designating him "the greatest *interpreter* of the spirit of Japanese life in Japanese landscape."[42] This *surimono,* dating from the late 1820s, measures 8 ⅝ x 7 ¼ in. The subject, a view of Mount Fuji, was closely associated with Hokusai, who was famous for his *ukiyo-e* series *The Thirty-six Views of Mount Fuji.* In this example, the poem in the upper left margin complements the image.

Dancing skylarks
sing at a pitch as high
as the tallest peak.

The hem of its skirt
wrapped in bands of mist –
Mount Fuji in the spring.[43]

NOTES

1. Randolph C. Henning, comp., *"At Taliesin": Newspaper Columns by Frank Lloyd Wright and the Taliesin Fellowship, 1934–1937* (Carbondale and Edwardsville: Southern Illinois University Press, 1992), 203.
2. Herbert Fritz, "At Taliesin," *An Uplands Reader* (April 1979): 139.
3. Edgar Tafel, *Apprentice to Genius: Years with Frank Lloyd Wright* (New York: McGraw-Hill, 1979), 148.
4. John Lloyd Wright, *My Father Who Is on Earth* (New York: G. P. Putnam's Sons, 1946), 43.
5. Ibid., 17.
6. Frank Lloyd Wright, *An Autobiography*, 2nd ed. (New York: Duell, Sloan and Pearce, 1943), 170.
7. Ibid., 187.
8. Dione Neutra, comp. and trans., *Richard Neutra, Promise and Fulfillment, 1919–1932* (Carbondale and Edwardsville: Southern Illinois University Press, 1986), 127.
9. F. L. Wright, *An Autobiography*, 260.
10. Frank Lloyd Wright to Lloyd Wright, January 8, 1931, Frank Lloyd Wright Archives, Taliesin West.
11. F. L. Wright, *An Autobiography*, 399.
12. Curtis Besinger, *Working with Mr. Wright: What It Was Like* (New York and Cambridge, England: Cambridge University Press, 1995), 18.
13. John Lloyd Wright, "Appreciation of Frank Lloyd Wright," *Architectural Design* 30 (January 1960): 2.
14. F. L. Wright, *An Autobiography*, 171.
15. Neutra, *Richard Neutra*, 127.
16. Besinger, *Working with Mr. Wright*, 80.
17. Henning, "At Taliesin," 219.
18. F. L. Wright, *An Autobiography*, 15.
19. *Taliesin Cookbook*, Frank Lloyd Wright Archives, Taliesin West.
20. Patrick J. Meehan, ed., *Frank Lloyd Wright Remembered* (Washington, D.C.: The Preservation Press, 1991), 182.
21. F. L. Wright, *An Autobiography*, 173.
22. Frank Lloyd Wright, "Living in the Desert, Part One – We Found Paradise," *Arizona Highways* 25 (October 1949): 12.
23. F. L. Wright, *An Autobiography*, 311.
24. Ibid., 454.
25. Philip Johnson, *Writings* (New York: Oxford University Press, 1979), 262.
26. Ibid., 198.
27. Besinger, *Working with Mr. Wright*, 85.
28. Ibid., 123.
29. Yukio Futagawa, ed., and Bruce Brooks Pfeiffer, text, *Frank Lloyd Wright, Selected Houses 3: Taliesin West* (Tokyo: A.D.A. Edita, 1989), 21.
30. J. L. Wright, "Appreciation," 3.
31. F. L. Wright, *An Autobiography*, 308.
32. Ibid., 452.
33. Ibid., 22.
34. John H. Howe, "Reflections of Taliesin," *Northwest Architect* 33 (July–August 1969): 26.
35. Ibid., 27.
36. J. L. Wright, *My Father*, 17.
37. F. L. Wright, *An Autobiography*, 174.
38. Ibid., 262.
39. Ibid., 263.
40. Ibid., 144–45.
41. Bruce Brooks Pfeiffer, ed., *Frank Lloyd Wright, Collected Writings, Volume 1, 1894–1930* (New York: Rizzoli International, 1992), 224.
42. Ibid., 223.
43. Joan Mirviss with John T. Carpenter, *The Frank Lloyd Wright Collection of Surimono* (New York and Phoenix: Weatherhill and Phoenix Art Musuem, 1995), 138.

SELECTED BIBLIOGRAPHY

Abernathy, Ann, and John Thorpe. *The Oak Park Home and Studio of Frank Lloyd Wright*. Oak Park, Illinois: Frank Lloyd Wright Home and Studio Foundation, 1988.

Barney, Maginel Wright. *The Valley of the God-Almighty Joneses*. New York: Appleton-Century, 1965. Reprint. Spring Green, Wisconsin: Unity Chapel Publications, 1986.

Besinger, Curtis. *Working with Mr. Wright: What It Was Like*. New York and Cambridge, England: Cambridge University Press, 1995.

Fritz, Herbert. "At Taliesin." *An Uplands Reader* (April 1979): 128–48.

Futagawa, Yukio, ed., and Masami Tanigawa, text. *Frank Lloyd Wright, Taliesin East, Spring Green, Wisconsin, 1925–; Taliesin West, Paradise Valley, Arizona, 1938–*. Tokyo: A.D.A. Edita, 1972.

Futagawa, Yukio, ed., and Bruce Brooks Pfeiffer, text. *Frank Lloyd Wright, Selected Houses 3: Taliesin West*. Tokyo: A.D.A. Edita, 1989.

———. *Frank Lloyd Wright, Selected Houses 2: Taliesin*. Tokyo: A.D.A. Edita, 1990.

Guerrero, Pedro E. *Picturing Wright: An Album from Frank Lloyd Wright's Photographer*. San Francisco: Pomegranate Artbooks, 1994.

Harrington, Elaine. *Frank Lloyd Wright Home and Studio, Oak Park*. Stuttgart: Edition Axel Menges, 1996.

Henning, Randolph C. *"At Taliesin": Newspaper Columns by Frank Lloyd Wright and the Taliesin Fellowship, 1934–1937*. Carbondale and Edwardsville: Southern Illinois University Press, 1992.

Howe, John H. "Reflections of Taliesin." *Northwest Architect* 33 (July–August 1969): 26–30, 63.

Kalec, Donald G. *The Home and Studio of Frank Lloyd Wright in Oak Park, Illinois, 1889–1911*. Oak Park, Illinois: Frank Lloyd Wright Home and Studio Foundation, 1982.

Lind, Carla. *Frank Lloyd Wright's Life and Homes*. San Francisco: Pomegranate Artbooks, 1994.

Meech-Pekarik, Julia. "Frank Lloyd Wright's Other Passion." In Carol R. Bolon, Robert S. Nelson, and Linda Seidel, eds. *The Nature of Frank Lloyd Wright*. Chicago: The University of Chicago Press, 1988.

Menocal, Narciso, ed. *Wright Studies I: Taliesin, 1911–1914*. Carbondale and Edwardsville: Southern Illinois University Press, 1992.

Mirviss, Joan, with John T. Carpenter. *The Frank Lloyd Wright Collection of Surimono*. New York and Phoenix: Weatherhill and Phoenix Art Museum, 1995.

Spirn, Anne Whiston. "Frank Lloyd Wright: Architect of Landscape." In David G. De Long, ed. *Frank Lloyd Wright: Designs for an American Landscape, 1922–1932*. New York: Harry N. Abrams, 1996.

Sweeney, Robert L. *Frank Lloyd Wright: An Annotated Bibliography*. Los Angeles: Hennessey & Ingalls, 1978.

Tafel, Edgar. *Apprentice to Genius: Years with Frank Lloyd Wright*. New York: McGraw-Hill, 1979.

Wiehle, Louis, ed. *Journal*. Los Angeles: Taliesin Fellows, 1990–present.

Wright, Frank Lloyd. *An Autobiography*. 2nd ed. New York: Duell, Sloan and Pearce, 1943.

———. *Frank Lloyd Wright: Letters to Apprentices*, Bruce Brooks Pfeiffer, ed. Fresno: The Press at California State University, 1982.

Wright, John Lloyd. *My Father Who Is on Earth*. New York: G. P. Putnam's Sons, 1946.

Wright, Olgivanna Lloyd. *Our House*. New York: Horizon Press, 1959.

———. *The Shining Brow: Frank Lloyd Wright*. New York: Horizon Press, 1960.

ACKNOWLEDGMENTS

It is impossible to mention by name all the individuals who have helped in the preparation of this work. However, special acknowledgment must be made to those without whom this book would never have been realized: the Frank Lloyd Wright Foundation, especially Richard Carney, Chairman of the Board, whose encouragement and support were given generously and often; the staff of the Frank Lloyd Wright Archives – Bruce Brooks Pfeiffer, Oscar Muñoz, Margo Stipe, Sara Hammond, and especially Penny Fowler, who has informed this book with her expert knowledge of Wright's art collection; the Taliesin Preservation Commission – Juli Aulik, Peter Rathbun, Ellen du Puy, and Bill du Puy; the Frank Lloyd Wright Home and Studio Foundation – Angela Fitzsimmons, Melanie Birk, and Gloria Garofalo. Taliesin, Taliesin West, and the Oak Park Home and Studio must speak for themselves, and the quality of Judith Bromley's photography allows the complexity of Wright's architecture to be captured in time. Her dedication and sensitivity under pressure are gratefully appreciated. It would be my desire to thank each member of the Taliesin Fellowship by name for the hospitality, generosity, and guidance that have been bestowed upon me during my countless visits to Arizona and Wisconsin. Alas, space does not permit. But both Minerva Montooth and Indira Berndston have graciously made me welcome on many occasions when it was especially difficult for them to do so, and John Rattenbury searched out rare photographs from his files. A word of thanks must go to Suzette Lucas and Serafino Garrella for assistance at Taliesin West and to Dirk Lohan for permission to publish the photograph of his grandfather Ludwig Mies van der Rohe. At Harry N. Abrams, Inc., I would like to acknowledge the enthusiasm of Paul Gottlieb and the careful attention of my editor, Diana Murphy, and the book's designer, Judith Hudson. My knowledge of Wright has been greatly augmented by instruction from so many colleagues. Special mention must be made of Donald Kalec, who opened his files and shared his knowledge of the Oak Park Home and Studio, Taliesin, and Taliesin West. I would also like to acknowledge the scholarship of Walter Creese, Neil Levine, Bruce Brooks Pfeiffer, Anthony Alofsin, Edgar Kaufmann jr., Narciso Menocal, and Thomas H. Beeby. Lastly to RHK, who has sustained me through the gestation of this book.

INDEX

PHOTOGRAPH CREDITS

The Art Institute of Chicago, Herbert and Katherine Jacobs Collection, Burnham Library: 21 bottom; copyright ©1997 Judith Bromley: 2, 4–5, 8, 16–19, 24, 29, 34–36, 40–44, 45 top, 46, 65–74, 77–79, 80–83, 86, 104–9, 110–14, 116–17, 129, 130, 134, 151; Chicago Historical Society: 15 top (HB-25942), 62 (HB-044414-V); copyright ©1997 Pedro E. Guerrero: 14 bottom, 20, 61; Maynard L. Parker Collection, The Huntington Library: 98 bottom, 99–101; John Rattenbury: 21 top, 23 top; Kathryn Smith: 56, 124 (top, collection author; middle and bottom, collection Donald Kalec), 125 (top, collection Donald Kalec; middle and bottom, collection author), 126 (collection author), 127 (collection Donald Kalec), 128 (collection Frank Lloyd Wright Foundation); State Historical Society of Wisconsin: 33 top (WHi[X3]23644), 57 top (WHi[X3]41629), 59 bottom (WHi[W6]28504); copyright ©1997

Taliesin Preservation Commission, Inc.: 64; John Howe Papers, Northwest Architectural Archives, University of Minnesota Libraries, St. Paul: 60; Manuscripts Division, University of Utah Libraries: 54 right; Arboretum, University of Wisconsin–Madison (photographed by Virginia Kline): 31 top left; The Frank Lloyd Wright Home and Studio Foundation: 30 top, 45 bottom; Frank Lloyd Wright Foundation: 10, 14 top, 15 bottom, 22, 23 bottom, 30 bottom, 31 top right, 31 bottom, 32, 33 bottom, 54 left, 55 triptych, 57 bottom, 58, 59 top, 63, 75, 76, 84, 93–97, 98 top, 102, 103, 115, 118–20, 132–33, 135 bottom (courtesy Lois Davidson Gottlieb), 156; Frank Lloyd Wright Foundation, collection Frank Lloyd Wright Foundation: 131, 135 top, 136, 140–50; copyright ©1997 Frank Lloyd Wright Foundation: 31 top right, 31 bottom, 33 bottom, 57 bottom, 76, 84, 103 bottom, 115, 120, 132–33; Scot Zimmerman: 6–7, 85

EDITOR: Diana Murphy
DESIGNER: Judith Hudson

LIBRARY OF CONGRESS
CATALOGING-IN-PUBLICATION DATA

Smith, Kathryn, 1945–
Frank Lloyd Wright's Taliesin and Taliesin
West / Kathryn Smith ; with photographs
by Judith Bromley.
      p.   cm.
Includes bibliographical references.
ISBN 0–8109–3991–6 (clothbound). —
ISBN 0–8109–2686–5 (Taliesin pb)
1. Wright, Frank Lloyd, 1867–1959—
Homes and haunts—Wisconsin—Spring
Green. 2. Wright, Frank Lloyd, 1867–
1959—Homes and haunts—Arizona—
Scottsdale. 3. Taliesin (Spring Green,
Wisc.) 4. Taliesin West (Scottsdale, Ariz.)
I. Title.
NA737.W7S433 1997
720' .92—dc21   96-49779

Copyright © 1997 Kathryn Smith

Published in 1997 by Harry N. Abrams,
Incorporated, New York
A Times Mirror Company

All rights reserved. No part of the contents
of this book may be reproduced without the
written permission of the publisher

Printed and bound in Japan

Harry N. Abrams, Inc.
100 Fifth Avenue
New York, N.Y. 10011
www.abramsbooks.com